KROWD

REVIEW

SPRING

2016

Editor-in-chief **Noga Sklar**
Literary editor **Rachel Hildebrandt**
Cover design **Bernardo Marçolla**
Cover illustration **Ernst Haeckel,** *Kunstformen der Natur, plate 99:*
Trochilidae, **1904**

ISBN: 978-1-944608-15-6
ISBN: 978-1-944608-14-9 (E-book)

www.krowdreview.com

KBR Digital Publishers LLC.
www.kbrdigital.com
www.facebook.com/kbrdigital
contact@kbrdigital.com

Greenville - SC
1|864|373.4528

LCO000000 Literary Collections

Hummingbirds (drawn from millinery specimens, body positions are not natural): (1) Male Ruby-throated Hummingbird; (2) Male Horned Sungem; (3) Male Crimson Topaz; (4) Male Red-tailed Comet; (5) Male Tufted Coquette; (6) Male Sword-billed Hummingbird; (7) Buff-tailed Sicklebill; (8) Male Dot-eared Coquette; (9) Male White-vented Violetear; (10) Male Hooded Visorbearer; (11) Female Juan Fernández Firecrown; (12) Male Booted Racket-tail.

SPRING
(LIFE / LOVE / LUST)

A Note From the Editor • 6

That Vision of Birds • 9
Bernardo Marçolla
Brazil

The Hands of My Father • 23
Wolfgang Hermann
Austria

Tandoori Nights • 27
Arnold Küsters
Germany

The Walking Philosopher • 43
Marcos Bulcão
Brazil

The Subversive Effects of Retirement • 57
Ana Cecília Carvalho
Brazil

Happiness is an Ecstatic Moment • 63
Noga Sklar
United States

Two Chimpanzees • 77
Marcelo Mirisola
Brazil

Beldade • 87
Francisco Inácio
Angola

A
NOTE
FROM
THE
EDITOR

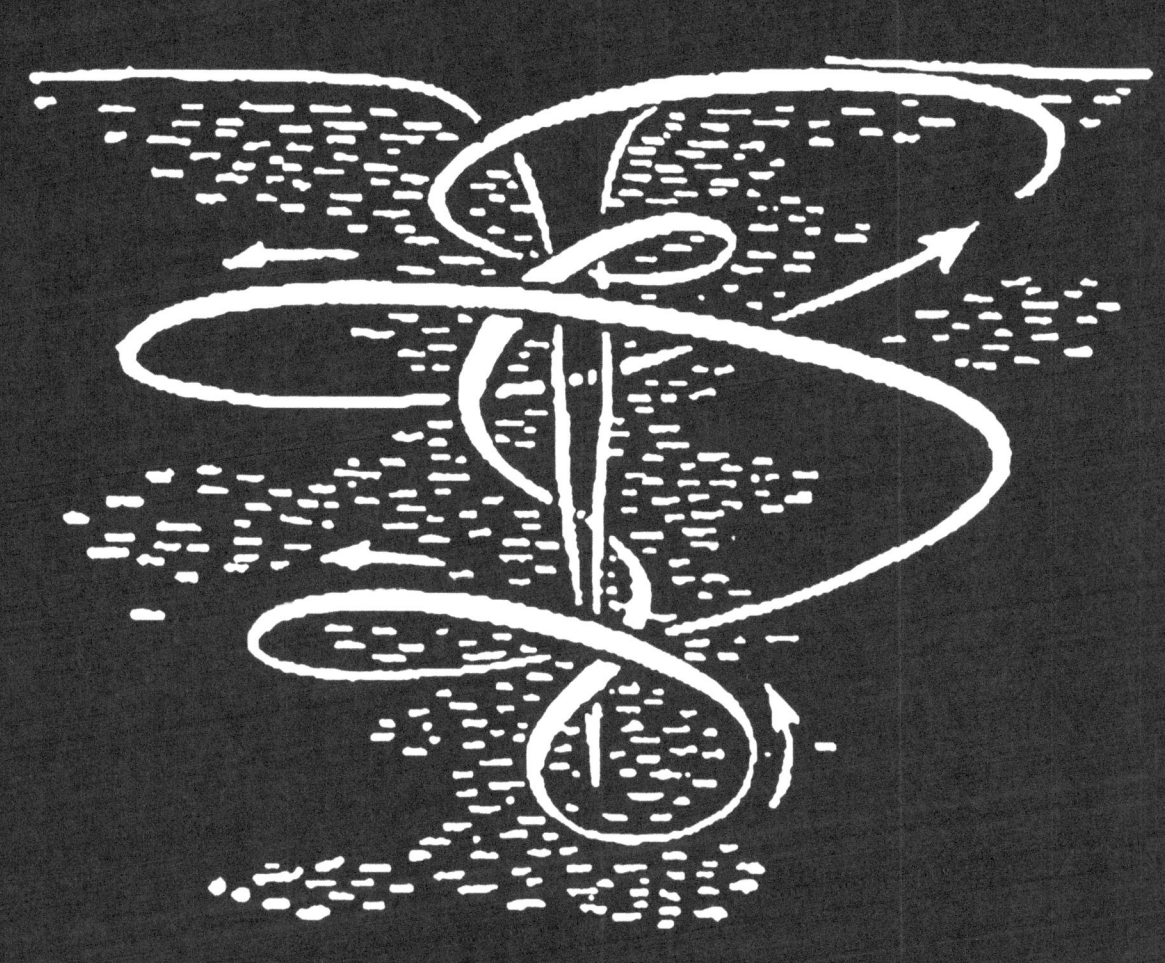

Dear Reader,

Spring is here, and the second edition of *Krowd Review* is dedicated to hummingbirds and other exotic fauna from the Brazilian lowlands, as lyrically reflected in the wildly flowered, exquisite prose of one of the most important Brazilian contributors to world literature, João Guimarães Rosa, beautifully analyzed by Bernardo Marçolla and translated by yours truly.

And that's not all. Since spring traditionally brings a seed of hope, this special edition intends to call your attention to a few wonderful books in translation — some of them already published, others available for publishing, others still awaiting a precious contribution that will allow them to flourish and make themselves known to the rest of the world, as is the case with our cover story, "That Vision of Birds."

Moreover, my husband Alan Sklar once told me that "art has a random element that comes from the unintended, the collective unconscious. It is magic, it is the universe talking through you." Therefore, not by coincidence, as I was working with this special edition I was not surprised to realize that the Chinese character for "spring" is also the one for "life, love and lust."

Each story in *Krowd Review #2 – The Spring Edition* is a wild journey in its own particular way. What they have in common is the ambition to take you along.

Welcome aboard!

That Vision of Birds[1]

Bernardo Marçolla
Brazil

---

1 Excerpt from the book *The Hummingbird Saga*. Rights in English available. Contact editor@kbrdigital.com.

Bernardo Marçolla holds a BA in psychology from the Pontifical Catholic University of Minas Gerais, Brazil (1997), a master's degree in psychology from the Federal University of Minas Gerais, Brazil (2000), a doctorate in literature by the Pontifícia Universidade Católica de Minas Gerais, Brazil (2006) and post-doctorate in Literature from the Federal University of Minas Gerais, Brazil (2010). He has worked for more than ten years as a teacher in the Department of Psychology in PUC-Minas. His experience in literature has an emphasis in the Brazilian iconic writer Guimarães Rosa and the development of the concept of "poetic porosity." His doctoral dissertation defended in 2006, which gave birth to his book *The Humminbird Saga* (KBR, 2015), received the CAPES award for Best Thesis of the year in the area of Arts in 2007.

*Translated by **Noga Sklar***

(Diadorim and the Life of the Soul)

Up to this point, I haven't truly occupied myself with Diadorim. This is the moment, the context being the relationship with the transcendental.

In many passages, the character Diadorim appears in association with birds.[2] There are occasions in which he is undifferentiated from them, others in which he teaches Riobaldo to connect with their beauty. I believe them to be flowing representations of the transcendental in GSV, producing a distinctive vision and also introducing the *presence of the soul*.

> Diadorim tripped on me, and as he cringed, he failed to understand me. Alive, a loner. Bird — he had such power. (GSV, p. 140)

> What was of value to me, even if brief and rare, was the way I feel, *remembrance and substance*. Those were the following, for example: *The Song of Siruiz; Bigri*, my mother, admonishing me; buriti, the palm tree — just like that, in clusters; the existence of *Diadorim*, the oddness of that gallant bird: *the killdeer*; the image of *Our Lady of Abbey*, a kind savior; *the little boys*, in the nude, not as angels are, behind their mothers, women seeking water at the river beach of the San Francisco, brimming buckets cushioned on their heads, no time for greater sorrows; and my *Otacilia* (emphasis added).

> In the silky thread of these memories, I think I was panning for *another sort of kindness* (emphasis added). (GSV, p. 391)

---

2 Albergaria (1977, p. 132) analyzes the presence of "winged creatures" in GSV, but, oddly, never refers to the birds.

In the previous passage, the author refers to "another sort of kindness," in contrast to the White-Wutu experience, full of memories and *substance* — the substance of affection, of art, of the transcendental, the beautiful. I call attention to the way in which each of these concrete references in Riobaldo's memories is a hybrid of the types of substances I have mentioned. When Riobaldo speaks of "a gallant bird," we can't be sure if he's referring to Diadorim or to the killdeer, that is, these two beings are merged into the hybrid "gallant bird." Diadorim himself is placed between the image of Our Lady and representations of nature (*buriti* palm tree, bird). Between Our Lady of Abbey and the boys in the river, we have the angels, which refer to both childhood and spirituality, again forming a hybrid. The women, the mothers of these angel-children who are in the river, lead to the memory of Otacilia. It should be noted that all this begins with a poetic intention — the *Song of Siruiz* — which leads to Mother Bigri, to the *buritis*, to Diadorim, to the killdeer, to the image of Our Lady of Abbey, to the children and their mothers, to Otacilia. The thread of memories does not end there; it does not end.

With regard to the killdeer, one should remember the exact moment when the bird is introduced to Riobaldo by Diadorim:

> The river, an object we so observed, with the yellow sandbank and a wide beach: come morning, it was refilled with a showing of birds. Renaldo himself caught my attention to it. What was common: these herons in a line, in all their whiteness; the jabiru; the green duck, the black duck, a crested duck; dancing drakes; kingfishers; mergansers; and even some vultures, in their sad tarnishing black. But, best of all — according to Renaldo — was the most beautiful and charming little bird up and down the river, the so-called killdeer.
>
> Until that time, I knew nothing of staring at them in joy, for the pleasure of their prettiness, of the mere life of them birds, in the starting and ending of their flights and landings. Those were meant to be hunted with a shotgun. But Renaldo enjoyed them, "graceful on their own," he

taught me. On the other side, marsh and ponds. All in all, flocks of ducks crossed in the air. "Watch these..." I looked, and it calmed me. (GSV, p. 111)

This passage also marks the reunion of "Renaldo" and Riobaldo, the moment when they start to reestablish a relationship that would include the exchanging of ideas and mutual learning; perhaps it was not a new beginning, but a continuation of what had begun in the crossing of the San Francisco, an eye-opening look at nature's beauty. Renaldo calls Riobaldo's attention to the birds, but in a new way: they are no longer hunting targets, but are to be targeted by the eye for their beauty and liveliness. Riobaldo is then reminded of nature's aesthetic character, its beauty and movement.

In the face of so much life and so many birds, Renaldo expresses his preference for *killdeers*,[3] always in pairs, "little male and female," a possible hint of the dual character in things, in himself. Could it be, on the other hand, also a clue about the appreciation of intersubjective dimensions, a ground on which Renaldo's friendship with Riobaldo could flower in such a way that the two of them could grow into a single being? This perspective is anticipated by Renaldo himself, when he recognizes the harmony between their two names:

> After this, we talked of tiny things others do not value. I was encouraged to speak of my life's arts, under unfocused light, to open myself in kindness, good. In everything I was pleased, no need to go further. *"Riobaldo... Renaldo..."* All of a sudden he burst out: "They form a pair, our two names..." We shared these words as a gift: for me, playing up what was already there, and joy; for him, a pinch of sadness. Why? I still did not know. (GSV, p. 112)

3 I recently had the opportunity to read a book on astronomy, in which I found out that the philosopher Immanuel Kant also devoted himself to physics and understood the galaxies as "island-universes" (Mourão, 2001, p. 187). The immediate association with the killdeer came to mind. This bird makes its nests on impermanent sand islands floating on rivers (of time?). Could this be a reference to Kant? This idea seems even more likely if we remember the philosopher's contributions to Aesthetics.

Diadorim, who always aligns himself with birds as we move through GSV, draws Riobaldo's attention to something that will prove to be essential in his path. This revelation is of such importance that Riobaldo even shares it with others, in this case, with Otacilia:

> And then, I spoke of the birds, busy with their flight before the haze. That vision of birds, that matter of God, it was Diadorim who had taught me. (GSV, p. 146)

The vision — *that vision of birds* — begins to emerge in the narrative as a possibility of transition and contact between different spheres of reality. This simple vision has great implications, but what does it mean?[4]

Riobaldo has premonitions, even if he does not see them as such at the time — neither does the reader, perhaps. They only acquire real meaning when confirmed at the end of the narrative. Shortly after his dialogue with Otacilia, Riobaldo anticipates Diadorim's death and the revelation that he is a woman:

> How can it be that I did not sense it? What about you, Mister? Can you imagine seeing the weightless, virgin body of a lass, killed by hand, stabbed, dyed by all its blood, the bloodless whiteness of the lips of her mouth, eyes set in a particular fashion, half-opened, half-closed? And that lass whom you loved, who was your destiny, the muffled and deaf hope of your life?! Oh, Diadorim... and so many years have passed. (GSV, p. 147)

This same movement is identified by Riobaldo as he structures

---

4 For Utéza (1994, p. 275), this vision is related to aesthetic learning, the purpose of which is to eliminate fear. The first lesson in harmony in this learning is conveyed through a ballet spectacle, in which the bird belongs both in the air and on Earth, in his "starting and ending of flights and landings." In parallel, the fusion of male and female elements is highlighted as well.

and proceeds with his narrative: he discusses not the fact itself, but the "thing-on-top," the "other-thing":[5]

> I beg you, Mister, to endure my wickedness into the storytelling. It's just ignorance. I don't talk to outsiders, almost never. I can't tell it right. I've learned a bit with my *compadre* Quelemem; but he wants to know everything in his own way: not the story as it came to be, but the thing-on-top, the other-thing. (GSV, p. 152)

After these reflections, Riobaldo resumes the account of the "concrete" journey he's on at this time. He dwells on the preparations and battles related to the fight against the Bebelos, while at the same time considering other topics relevant to the thread that I'm following here.

Riobaldo speaks about walking at night, explaining how one can transcend the absence of light — which brings me back to the limited awareness linked to ordinary levels of reality, as if the material in nature were a dark night. Once this is established, here are his seeing strategies:

> One has to get used to the dark in one's eyes. I'm telling you everything, Mister. Our walking was measured in silence, not even the step of the sandals was heard. From those low bushes that kill, the buzzing of the bugs denoted a million. There the great owl flies, it knows exactly where it goes, knows no noise. When its shadow haunted us in the air, I closed my eyes three times. (GSV, p. 156)

> What if there was any danger arising there, and I reaped the alert? That was quite often the case. I knew; I've heard. Gunmen who take this gift often guess what's about to come, so in good time they escape. Like Hermogenes. John Goanha, of all people, was susceptible to such hunches out of thin air, forespoken. Was this true for me? (GSV, p. 167)

---

5 In terms of GSV's literary reviews, that which Riobaldo calls the "bad inquest into the storytelling" has been explored by Márcia Marques de Morais (2001) within the framework of psychoanalytic assumptions. From this perspective, these images may acquire meanings quite different from the ones I'm pointing out.

This ability to guess is part of the gunman's art. In close contact with matter, they catch these "hunches out of thin air, forespoken." These strategies subsumed into the extraordinary reveal themselves with more and more refinement, even though they are described through the merging with what we see in the ordinary world. Riobaldo listens to "other" birds:

> Many a time we moved on through tracks in the woods, tapir footsteps — back and forth... At night, if it's to be, heavens lump together a glow. Our head almost bumps into it. Beautiful as can be, like the starry sky in mid-February. But, when there's no moon, in the dark that's there, it's a fearful darkness, which stops and gets you. A quantity of night. The total blackness in the drylands always made me sick. Not Diadorim, no, he would stick to the flaming ice of that concept; he had no concerns. But I wished dawn to come. Hot day, cold night. We would pick some vellozia to light a fire. If we could eat and drink, I could fall asleep. I dreamed. Only dreams, good or bad, rather. I had in me a hidden moon. At the break of day, *I listened to different birds.* Kingbirds, blackbirds, ground-doves, *white-tipped* doves, *ruddy* quail-doves. And then the kiskadee. Behind and ahead of me, all around me, it seemed to be *a lonely* kiskadee. *"Gee! You don't find one until you find out it's unique. Right?" I asked Diadorim* (emphasis added). (GSV, pp. 27-28)

The tapir's footsteps, "back and forth," refers to a rhythm, the composition of the verse. Could this be the entrance, in the direction of what might be? The idea this passage transmits to me is that of movement and transition into the extraordinary, along the paths of nature. Moreover, at the break of the day, you could hear *different* birds. Riobaldo mentions those that appear at the crack of dawn — *kingbirds, blackbirds, ground-doves, white-tipped doves, ruddy quail-doves, kiskadees* — but without specifying which were the *different* ones he had heard earlier, or *which* he had heard, birds of dreams.

About these other ones, weren't they the same ones? This is reflected in the combined names of the birds, on top of the language substrate, which can be understood in either an ordinary or an extraordinary manner, the hidden message, anticipatory, "visionary": The white chest, which becomes ruddy when the gentle maiden is killed... Then it becomes clear. Diadorim: was he always one and the same? I guess not. Inherent to the words is a permeability which crosses through time, through dimensions and levels of consciousness. I call your attention, once again, to the creation of a vision associated with birds, which breaks the boundaries between time and space.

At a later point in the narrative, shortly before the beginning of the great battle, Riobaldo, "riding the moment" (GSV, p. 418), still has time to be ashamed of himself and to point out that Diadorim "was not mortal." Moreover, Diadorim's presence did not abide by his rules. Could that be a recognition of Diadorim's soul — *or of Diadorim as a soul* — transcending form and matter?

The next day, Riobaldo receives the news that Hermogenes is approaching. At the same time, Trigoso speaks of a cowboy who had reported seeing a man named Abram, with a well-dressed girl. Wondering if it could be Otacilia and with the intention of protecting her, Riobaldo heads in their direction in the company of Alaripe and Quipes. Fairly shaken, Riobaldo refers to Renaldo as "Diadorim" for the first time in front of the gunmen (GSV, p. 429) — until then this name was a secret well-kept between them both. This is the first time the name is uttered, creating an immediate association with the name of a bird:

> But then, I uncovered what was hidden, giving up the past, I could not care less; therefore, I explained: "Diadorim" is Renaldo... Alaripe was silent, to better understand. But Quipes laughed: "Dindurinh... A good nickname... He made it sound like a passerine, the name of a bird." (GSV, p. 429)

Here I emphasize the importance of naming Diadorim — giving soul a name. Then, in reference to the alleged presence of Mister Habao and Otacilia at that place, Riobaldo remembers the stone incident:

"Mister Habao handed her the amethyst stone..." I said. I said it out loud; and I didn't want Alaripe to echo me: "...handed her the stone." That is: the stone was a topaz! Only as I recount it, I make a mistake, this change — that's how confused I get. Diadorim suffered most of all, I guess, because of the endowing of that stone. (GSV, p. 430)

Dowering, owing, "endowing" — it is interesting that Riobaldo refers to the fact that the stone's name was changed: amethyst or topaz, the change is attributed to a mistake when recounting the story. But let us look, because the change is significant, since it's not only the stone's recipient who changes — Diadorim to Otacilia. Even the stones themselves can be transformed: tourmaline (p. 48), topaz (p. 49), sapphire (p. 282), "stone of value" (p. 334), and amethyst (pp. 430 and 454). This refers once more to the "scoring" process I have mentioned before, to the possibility of dislocating the senses as one tells a story. Even a stone can change.[6] However, I do not see this change as a mistake, but as the creation of new senses. Riobaldo speaks of how the art of storytelling gives life even to stones...

Because it was the eve of the awaited day: look see. But this thing, so upright, so close, was still clouded, hidden in the future. Who knows what this surrounding stone material is heating, that in due time, from within its hardness, will form *a newborn bird*? (emphasis added) (GSV, p. 425)

I examine the image of this stone so exactly because it acquires a life of its own: was it an egg, this stone that changes when heated? Could that stone egg also be a *crystal ball*, enclosing the seed of the future? In this way, we are pointed toward an extensive associative chain of signifiers: *Diadorim bird vision soul stone that changes egg*. Will the premature death of Diadorim be accompanied by a birth? Riobaldo envisions how transformed his perception of life's

---

6 Utéza (1994, p. 121) refers to the "floating" character of this stone.

"ordinary" things really is, "discoupled" from other people's perception and feelings.

I believe we can summarize many of the ideas in this context through the realization that *the contact with the extraordinary happens through the creation of a vision,*[7] a soul vision. When touched by something that transcends the ordinary reality of things, Riobaldo becomes a visionary, a possibility that has been foreshadowed since the beginning of his narrative. As I already mentioned, at one point, Riobaldo reveals: "*That vision of birds*, that matter of God, it was Diadorim who had taught me" (emphasis added) (GSV, p. 146). Perhaps this passage constitutes an important starting point for the issues I now intend to address: What could be the relationship between the creation of this vision and literature? And arts in general?

Let's see. In the first place, under the perspective of a visionary, *that vision of birds* would be a double one. This vision can be understood as the capacity of seeing the way birds see — from the heights, as a "matter of God," transcendental and extraordinary. Diadorim, in fact, initiates Riobaldo into a communion with nature, in such a way that his world (and also his being) expands greatly. It is possible to see things differently, "spiritually"; the doors to which ordinary eyes cannot see are thus opened. On the other hand, this same vision can also be understood as the power to see what you could not see before, but which has always been there: The birds only gain real substance for Riobaldo once Diadorim names them. In other words, *vision* could also refer to the uttered word, and maybe this is the role played by art: the representation and denomination of the ineffable.

These two dimensions in fact complement each other. As you can see, there is a close relationship between the one who names (and who has the vision) and that which is named (and which is seen). Both visionary and vision are incorporated in the bird in such a way that there seems to be a sort of communion between the subject and the world, which refers to something ineffable narrated by Riobaldo

---

7 Others have addressed the role of visions in Rosa's body of work. Melania Aguiar (2001), whom I mentioned earlier, dedicates herself explicitly to this dimension when analyzing the short stories in *Tutameia*.

while telling his experience of the pact. In this sense, could "that vision of birds" be an aesthetic experience?

In the context of these elements, it is clear that the word occupies a central place when confronted with the *vision*. I call attention to the articulation of the "ineffable" present in the alleged "pact with the devil": maybe the attempt to retrieve power, identity, and meaning is facilitated through the attempt to articulate the word. Throughout Rosa's *Grande sertão: veredas* we are continually pointed toward the power of the name — of a person's name, of the names of animals and things, of locations - names which are mutant and alive. It is possible to take ownership of anything, provided one can give it a name. Riobaldo receives all the birds as a gift when Diadorim draws his attention to their existence and teaches him their names; then, and only then, do they begin to be seen.

Here we have the intricate relationship between a *vision* and the corresponding representation created through a word. The *vision* could be an invitation, a call related to the function of literature, an invitation to articulation — not just the articulation of words already expressed in the narrative, but all articulations made possible from the day the text began encountering its possible readings and potential readers.

These thoughts do not disregard the image of birds associated with the *vision*. Shamanic journeys, marked in essence by visionary experiences, are often described as flights of the soul: the bird finally sees himself. Ryan (1999, p. 9) uses the image of the eye to refer to these experiences; for him, while Westerners obsessively look "outside," the shamans develop what is called by Australian aborigines a "strong" or "inside" view — "the strong eye." The articulation of the word seems to possess the same power. We can then ask ourselves: Are we the ones reading a book, or is the book reading us?

In addition to flying, birds also sing. Therefore, as he articulates the word, the visionary is acting not as a composer, but as an instrument, through which music can be expressed — as in Riobaldo's "breeze of the sacred" and "endless stars" (GSV, p. 319). When talking about the "death of the author," Barthes (1990, p. 228) makes this same reference to the shaman (the visionary) as a mediator of language, narrating something that does not emanate out of himself.

In his essay *Profane Illuminations (Poets, Prophets and Drug Addicts)*, José Miguel Wisnik (1995) discusses the visionary experience as a subject which is simultaneously very old and extremely contemporary. Referring to the ties that bind visionary and poetic experiences, Wisnik exposes a foundational dimension: the "metaphysical" is not dissociated from everyday experience. Art, therefore, "*is and is not from another world*," as Riobaldo would say.

Wisnik leads us to the fundamental conclusion that every visionary experience relates to a poetic expression. And I believe this can provoke a reversal of considerations. We could ask if certain poetic expressions we encounter on an ordinary basis may actually originate as visionary experiences.

What arises, then, is the controversy around the genesis of some works of art, which is very common in the context of the scholarly criticism that surrounds Guimarães Rosa: Does his writing result from deliberate work or from metaphysical inspiration? For Wisnik, however, this separation is deluded and historically conditioned:

> Confronted with the enigma, the sacred calls its dazzling by the name of God, while the profane labels the same dazzling as emptiness and random chance. Modern prophecy is the frailly tangential and vanishing line between these two conceptions. They differ as conceptions and also in their consequences (modernity being the desacralizing split at the foundation of this divergence). As a vision, from which the aesthetic considerations originate, these two conceptualizations can be merged (since the contradiction between the sense of the transcendental and the lack of sense is not exclusionary in visionary logic). (Wisnik, 1995, pp. 297-298)

For Wisnik, the vision is no longer associated with the sacred; it is no longer bound to rite or myth, nor is it part of the profane, as it refuses to adopt current and visible language as its form of articulation. The vision can be conceived as a fleeting apparition, seated on a "missing column;" within this framework, the boundaries between the ordinary and the extraordinary seem to become less rigid.

Thus, in the context of GSV, "that vision of birds" apparently refers to the "presence of a hummingbird":

But it turns out that the moment between sleep and wakefulness was fairly short, it just passed by, you could not stand in it. I could not take a firm stand on anything, clarity ceased immediately. Through those warnings and intentions, the rising tide of the world dissolved me, sucked me dry. And the rest of the time, I was opposed to myself. Wasn't I? The gunmen were all growing increasingly obedient to me with each passing day, exalting me more and more. Because of that, I got into the habit of jump out of my hammock in an instant, as if to avoid that extra bit of beneficial intelligence that seemed to be coming from the bottom of my heart. A sudden leap, and it was gone — a loose spark, the presence of a hummingbird, which is gone a second after its arrival — I was already back to common sense, to a halfway heart: a half-goodness mixed with half-evil. Now that I was up, I harnessed and mounted my Siruiz, a morning horse. And left the camp all by myself. (GSV, p. 371)

Could that be an aesthetic experience?

The Hands of My Father

Wolfgang Hermann
Austria

Born in 1961 in Bregenz, Austria, **Wolfgang Hermann** studied philosophy in Vienna, after which he traveled extensively and lived in Berlin, Paris, Aix en Provence, and Tokyo. He has published numerous books of prose and poetry, among the most recent: *Abschied ohne Ende* (novel, 2012), *Schatten auf dem Weg durch den Bernsteinwald* (poetry, 2013), *Die Kunst des unterirdischen Fliegens* (novel, 2015), and *Die letzten Gesänge* (stories, 2015). Wolfgang Hermann's numerous prizes include the Juergen Ponto Prize (1987), the Siemens Literature Prize (2002), the Anton Wildgans Prize (2006), and the Austrian State Advancement Award (2007). *Herr Faustini takes a Trip* is the first of his books published in English.

*Translated by **Mark Miscovich***

My father, who fought for every handbreadth of life right up to the end, lay slack in his bed under the influence of morphine one evening a few weeks before his death. He had loosened his grip on the trapeze handle and lay there on this early autumn evening in the realm between this and another world. He mumbled a few unconnected words to himself, and I thought he hadn't noticed me when he turned toward me and with hazy eyes whispered, "Can you cut my fingernails?"

Ever since my childhood, physical contact between my father and I had been limited to a firm handshake. Maybe, when he was in a good mood, he might have patted me on the shoulder once.

I took his cadaverous hand and was astonished to find that it felt like soft leather. My father opened his eyes, but wasn't able to focus on me, his eyes turning up toward another realm. I held in my hand the softened leather hand of a man who had gone through nearly a century with this hand. It was the hand of a strong man, one who, no matter where he was, instantly gained respect through his bold and confident air. Now, this hand wanted to rest and let go of the reins. It entrusted itself to me for the very first time in my life. My hand couldn't simply hold the hand of this strong, dying man. It needed the nail scissors as a bridge. And with care and gratitude it cut the fingernails of the hand of my father, in whom a spark of life still flickered. I not only cut the nails of this hand, I embarked on a journey to an unknown land. I cut the nails of this hand which I had feared like no other. With a small gesture this hand had decided for weal or woe. It had done this with such an authority that none of us had ever questioned it. Now, this hand lay in mine and besides the clipped nails, something like a dark light surged through these fingers. I saw it flow through both of our hands: into this frail body waiting on its last breath, and into the body of the son who had waited for it for so long.

Tandoori Nights

Arnold Küsters
Germany

Arnold Küsters was born in 1954, in Breyell, a village that is now part of Nettetal. His father was a master butcher, like his grandfather before him, and his mother was a trained milliner. Arnold studied English and pedagogy in Siegen. He was a journalist at the *Westdeutsche Zeitung*, and worked in both radio and television at Westdeutscher Rundfunk. For more than 10 years he has also worked as a PR and press agent. As a member of the Syndicat, the union of the German-speaking crime writers (Germany, Austria, and Switzerland), Küsters has published a number of crime & mystery novels and participated in short-stories anthologies.

Also a musician, Arnold Küsters plays the harp in "Hands Up!" — the only "crime writers blues band" in the world, and was awarded the Krefeld Short Crime Prize in 2009.

Translated by **Brian Jenkins**

I looked at my watch. How much longer was he going to keep me waiting?

I'm talking about Paddy O'Brien, one-time kitchen hand and occasional cook at the Big House. I had met Paddy exactly twenty-one years ago to the day. I'd once had the hots for him, or more accurately for his athletic Irish arse. Yes, those were hot times, but long gone. The Big House is no longer the pride of the glorious British army. To be honest, the streets and buildings of Joint Headquarters are well past their best, and the same goes for Paddy's backside. As he rapidly established himself as an authority on British fish'n'chips shops, his hindquarters lost their muscle tone at similar breathtaking speed. That much I could tell from the occasional photos in the *Daily Mail* or the *Daily Telegraph*.

Alright, I'll admit that at first there were still one or two sentimental moments when I asked myself what had become of those three square-shaped freckles at the top of his right thigh. But, as I said, it was all long ago.

At some stage, we'd lost touch. It's often that way in the army. A new posting comes along- it's the same anywhere the soldiers of the Queen get sent.

Basically I was happy things had turned out that way. That chalk-white, red-haired Irishman could be a real pest, especially when he'd had a skinful. Then Paddy would think he was Shane MacGowan, from the prole folk-punk band The Pogues, and he would growl out the old songs. Frankly a worn-out juke-box had a good deal more style than he did!

I would have ended our relationship anyway, if you can call it a relationship, what with Paddy's obsessive desire to have me all to himself. Because it so happened that my unit had a few things planned for me, where Paddy would have been an obstacle. In short, Paddy soon left the Army, while I underwent special training which allowed me, under the alias of Shiva Kruger, to take on assignments which required more than just muscle power.

I think the Joint Staff found it amusing to give me the pseudonym Shiva. My mother was from a village on the western coast of India, and my father was stationed for a while in various Indian federal states. I was born at some point.

Anyway, my skin color made me ideal for special assignments, whether in the Balkans, Afghanistan or Iraq. The missions soon began to resemble one another, like peas in a pod, and the slack time between deployments differed only in the degree of boredom involved. The passing months had long since lost any meaning, and the years rushed through my life like the sand on a dusty desert track. In the end, I no longer knew exactly which country I was in, exactly which day it was, or exactly which targets I had to eliminate. All that mattered to me was a successful outcome followed by a free weekend.

One morning I woke up in some camp or other, and found myself missing the children I didn't have. That was the day I got out. It was decided in the blink of an eye. I was the best, but they just had to accept it.

I then tried living a normal life. A nine-to-five office job in a small tourist information bureau on the market square in Stow, in the Cotswolds, west of London. The work was easy, and I was popular with colleagues and customers alike, thanks to my familiarity with foreign languages. Every Wednesday evening, with my very nice but frankly rather simple-minded coworkers, I went to the fitness sessions at the church hall. Thursday evenings was Bingo; Fridays was the pub round the corner. Suddenly my life was running on quite different and rigidly controlled lines. I had established a routine for myself, but this same pattern day after day made me sleepy. I felt like a salamander dozing on the hot stones in the midday heat of Nevada.

To be honest, I was bored stiff, and I longed for some variety. For the job itself was OK. Only Veronica, with whom I shared my shifts, wished me luck when I handed in my notice. I told her I was taking a creative break, thanks to a small inheritance. When I remarked that I was not going to disappear and would stay living in Stow-on-the-Wold, she responded with a brave smile.

I have no idea exactly how they found me. One rainy afternoon, a man in wet hiking gear was suddenly standing there at the tourist information counter, asking for a couple of worthwhile walking routes. I did not yet know at that moment that he called himself Clark Kent, that he worked for a company hitherto completely unknown to me, an Anglo-Indian chicken meat consortium, and that he would be my contact in all my future operations. And of course, I never suspected that, in less than six months, I would be seeing Paddy O'Brien again.

Chicken meat consortium! A likely story! Of course, I didn't believe him. Or his "Clark Kent"! It could be that the German Federal Intelligence Service was behind it all, or one of the Chinese triads, or the Russian Mafia. I didn't care. The main thing was, here was a change, and the money was right.

My first 'job' was the thing in Coverack, in Cornwall. The fish'n'chips shop right on the harbor. The Old Lifeboat House. A nice place actually. Popular, good fish, fresh oil, good reputation.

I had been super-prepared. In black leather and helmet, I rode the black Suzuki along the village street, which gave a wide vista of the bay and the open sea.

The bazooka pierced the fish counter without difficulty. Long before the fireball of explosives mixed with cod and vegetable oil had turned the white-washed, former lifeboat station into a baking-hot oven with more than fish smeared on the walls, I was already on my way. Above the village, I destroyed the bike and leather with some hefty explosives and disappeared down the coast path towards Cadgwith. A reasonably attractive woman in her mid-forties with high cheekbones, very dark eyes, and — as everyone told me later — a slightly Indian look, who did not look her real age, even at second glance.

Unfortunately, the operation did not go entirely smoothly. The bazooka had presumably been a touch too powerful. As they said later on the radio, the village had been seriously affected by this "terrible attack out of the blue." Many years of preservation work on a unique historical site had been wiped out forever in the space of a few seconds. "And for what, for God's sake?" This was the question that no one could answer, neither the horrified commentators nor the various Detective Chief Inspectors nor the grieving bereaved of the customers and owners of the shop. Not to mention myself.

My clients were not exactly happy about the alleged disaster, for which I was supposedly responsible. My instructions had been to be swift and effective. That was what I had been hired to do. Frying innocent people and blowing up half the village was not part of the agreement. What did I have to say about that?

Little. Even my honest admission that, after all these years, I might be a little out of practice, and that the Coverack special assignment was a somewhat unfortunate dummy run, failed to convince them. Because I still had pride in myself as a professional, I guaranteed that all future operations would go without a hitch. I would simply need a little time. At least I still got the promised fee.

In the operations that followed with increasing frequency, I took greater care. In Penzance, number 2, things went better. The Market Place Fish Bar. The high counter was no real problem. I just used the Colt M1911 that my father had left me. Honestly! The red-cheeked woman with the bleached short hair and her fat friend didn't have a chance.

From assignment to assignment, my confidence grew. And whenever I carried the old pistol, I always felt close to Daddy. My father had bought the M1911 and silencer from an American, not long after the end of the Vietnam War.

Soon I was back in my old rhythm. Clark would leave the envelope with the necessary information behind the mirror in the ladies' restroom at the Queen's Head Inn in Stow. I was always well-prepared, and presto, a light touch on the trigger, pft, pft, and almost of their own accord two bullets from the M1911 were drilled into the target body. Always just two: one would have been enough, the second was just to be on the safe side.

Sure, now and then there was the odd mishap that could probably have been avoided, like the Coverack thing, but as time went by the finger practice also produced some real masterpieces.

I could have been happy and content if only my patrons had seen things the same way. They always managed to find something wrong with my work. Sometimes the timing had been bad, because there were still customers in the shop. Sometimes they even claimed it was the wrong fish'n'chips shop on the wrong day.

I asked Clark Kent about it. Who exactly were these people whose dirty work I was doing at considerable risk? And why precisely were owners of fish'n'chips shops the targets for my M1911? But the longer I worked for the "Family," as Clark called his bosses, the more reticent he became. He was the contact man. He gave me my assignments and my money. End of story! And always the reminder to be more professional next time. I was under scrutiny. The slightest mistake, and I was out. And I could surely imagine "exactly what that meant." With this, in true film gangster style, he tapped the lapel of his jacket in a meaningful way. What a prick!

They could, on the other hand, have been very proud of me. There was prime-time coverage on television. The papers were full of the continuing story. "How much longer must fish'n'chips merchants face sudden death?" chorused the headlines over a series of articles in the *Daily Mail*.

A national debate was launched over the nutritional value of haddock, cod or plaice when combined with fatty chips, salt and vinegar. In Parliament, the MPs were no longer unanimous in opposing fishing quotas in the future. In the meantime, the Prime Minister had a rough ride. In short, I had stirred things up well and truly, but clearly there was still something that was upsetting my clients. And I hadn't the faintest idea what it could be.

Or indeed, as I've said, why it had to be these specific fish'n'chips shops. However, I didn't ask any more questions. One fish'n'chips shop is much like any other: handwritten blackboard announcing which varieties of fish were on offer, semi-thawed chips, fat, flour, aluminum salt cellars, vinegar bottles, aprons of varying degrees of cleanliness.

All I knew, or, to be more precise, what I came to suspect a little more each day, was that my clients were becoming increasingly nervous about me and my work. And yet my "error-quota," as they insisted on calling the occasional little slip-up, was close to zero. After all, I'd given up using unwieldy devices like bazookas and mortars, in favor of matches or my well-oiled M1911. In fact, I had gone out of my way to satisfy my clients. However, in all events there was always a Plan B. I could simply get out of the trade without delay. This pragmatic approach to life was something I had inherited from my Indian mother, who was of course familiar with the concept of karma. A legacy that pleased me, like Daddy's pistol.

I was prepared. For quite some time, I had had the sensation that, in the darkness, thousands of eyes were staring at me through my window. And before I climbed into my old Honda, I checked the ground plate.

My own karma had come into play only two days ago. I felt it in the morning, during my daily workout. Kent's phone call, as always, took me by surprise. I simply could not get used to the shrill tone of the old telephone in my little home.

"Clark here."

How unnecessary. Nobody else knew my number.

"A special assignment this time."

Weren't all the others special too?

"Don't screw it up! Everything depends on it. It's vital. This time my bosses won't tolerate any mistakes. Explanations and excuses won't wash."

Somewhere in his voice there was guilt, and this made the hairs stand up on the back of my neck. I nodded hesitantly, though of course Clark Kent couldn't see me.

"Shiva?"

"Yes, anything else?"

"Further details behind the mirror, as usual."

"And then?"

"What?"

"What if I screw up?"

In reply, I heard him tap the lapel of his jacket.

After this memorable phone call, I took a short walk across the square to my dead letter box in the *Queen's Head* and, after taking an alibi pee, retrieved my envelope from behind the mirror. I had ripped it open and read it before I'd even crossed the square. What I saw hit me like a thunderbolt from a clear sky.

In the bar, I let them pour me a Donnington ale, just to get me halfway back on my feet. It was also to get my brain working. When the landlord shoved the pint across the counter, he looked at me as if I was pregnant and really shouldn't be drinking.

I merely shrugged and took my beer outside to sit on a bench underneath the pub sign with its stern image of Elizabeth I. I put my beer down, and pulled the envelope out from under my t-shirt. Three pictures, each of them showing Paddy O'Brien. As I've said, no longer quite so muscular as when I had known him, older of course, and with a lot less hair. In one of them, Paddy was standing in an ancient pub with dangerously low ceilings, grinning as he held his beer glass aloft. Another showed him in a fish'n'chips shop, and the third was of O'Brien at a book-signing for his best-seller *The Ultimate Guide to Britain's Most Famous Fish'n'Chips Shops Ever*.

An accompanying note gave Paddy's birth-and-death dates, along with the arrival time of a National Express bus in Stow-on-the-Wold. Stow. Did it really have to be here?

As I said, that was nearly forty-eight hours ago. Since then, I've hardly closed my eyes, but I did have a plan. And I had stripped down my M1911 five times in succession, oiled it and reassembled it. It was as good as new.

Now I sat, on that Tuesday, in Stow-on-the-Wold outside my local, the *Queen's Head*, hoping that Veronica would not suddenly run across the road to greet me and watching the dusty street over the rim of my beer glass. Right on time, the National Express bus swung into view, stopped a few meters from the pub, and disgorged Paddy O'Brien, swaying with a travel bag in his hand. He was as drunk as a rugby team after a victory over the All Blacks. The Irishman really hadn't changed at all. He put his bag down, waved to the bus, and softly hummed "For he's a jolly good fellow," all the while smiling and shaking his head. He turned around, picked up the bag, and stopped in mid-movement. He had seen me.

"Cheers." I raised my glass. You poor drunken Mick. You're going to get off your head. If necessary in the *Queen's Head.* And in less than ten hours, you will be one very dead Irishman.

"Hi, love." O'Brien's face did not reveal whether he was surprised to see me in Stow.

"Paddy." I took a deep draught of beer.

He remained standing before me, uncertain. "Are you OK?"

"Fine."

"Do you still smoke?" O'Brien searched for his cigarettes in his jacket.

I noted dear Paddy's discomfort with satisfaction. "No, too dangerous."

Paddy merely nodded. He eyed me with a mixture of suspicion and curiosity. "You have business here?"

"Of course."

"That's good." Paddy seemed to have decided that a bit of conversation was appropriate in this situation.

I took another draught and now looked at him myself with a bit more care. Curiously, he suddenly seemed a good deal less drunk that he had a few moments ago, when he was taking leave of his new friends. I decided to proceed more cautiously.

"Another one?" He pointed to my almost empty glass and was already off into the pub without waiting for my answer. "It's my birthday today."

Why not? It would be his last after all. I followed him and sat down by one of the two windows. I didn't want to let him open the conversation.

"What exactly are you doing in Stow?" I asked him. The pub was not very busy. A couple of farmers at the bar, discussing their bad luck on the horses, a pair of Japanese tourists on custom-made low stools, leafing through travel guides. So there was no danger that our conversation would attract unwelcome attention.

"I could ask you the same thing," said Paddy. "What a strange coincidence. But never mind. Let's talk about old times. Cheers, Debbie."

"You didn't answer my question. Won't you sit down?" I raised my glass in silent response to his "Cheers."

O'Brien remained standing, looking down at me. He lowered his voice. "You won't believe me, but it's about the future of fish'n'chips."

I shook my head in disbelief. Paddy always was a head case. Perhaps the idea of having a last drink together wasn't such a good one after all.

"Leave it be. I know you're a really big name in the business. Hardly a bookshop window that doesn't have your bestseller on display."

O'Brien drew up a stool and sat down, all serious. He looked furtively around before continuing. "I'm here virtually incognito. That's what that act was about earlier. I deliberately took the bus. Pure self-preservation. Nobody can know I'm here. I have a mission to accomplish. On her Majesty's service."

"Paddy, stop this nonsense. Let's go." I took a long pull on my pint. "On her Majesty's service." I mimicked his tone. "And from the mouth of an Irishman no less!" I wanted to get the whole thing over. Paddy really was a pretentious asshole.

But O'Brien wasn't listening. He sipped nervously at his beer, looking me steadily in the eye. "I shouldn't really tell you. But as the two of us have, hmm, known each other for such a long time, I don't think I'm making a mistake."

I rolled my eyes, but that didn't stop him.

"You've heard about all these attacks?"

I said nothing.

"So far all the shops that have been hit are on my list of the best in the country."

I took a sip of beer. This was getting interesting. "And what's that got to do with Stow?"

"The police think that if I nominate *Greedy's*, down there on Park Street, as the current no.1 fish'n'chips shop in the world, they might set a trap for the perpetrator. And besides, the Indian restaurant *Prize of India* is just down the road."

"What have Indians got to do with it?" I was on the defensive. "Perpetrator?"

"Yep. Male. About 25. That's what they've put together from witness statements and profiling. One of these characters who spends the whole day on the internet and who thinks the world was created so that they could play Counterstrike in real life, and thereby ensure that they can live exclusively on pizza or Chicken Tikka Masala."

"Internet? Chicken Tikka?" I leaned back and enjoyed the next draught. I knew now that I was still the master of my trade. So they were looking for some overweight nerd who knew nothing about the world, let alone fish'n'chips.

"Don't laugh. It's much more serious than you think. The authorities are really worried." To give his words more weight, Paddy drew himself up to his full height, which didn't mean that much in his case.

I shrugged my shoulders and let him talk.

"The fishing lobby has a lot of influence. The national heritage is at stake. Just imagine," he spoke like a lecturer addressing his students, "this chicken curry thing has knocked fish'n'chips off the podium as our national dish. Our national identity will disappear down the Thames if we don't do something. It's unbelievable. Nowadays more people are eating this spicy crap than my lovely fries and batter."

He looked at me as if he had just announced that in two days the world would run out of oxygen. And I was indeed stunned. So that was the way the wind was blowing. I was stuck in the middle of a bitter war over British eating habits. Now I could finally see the significance of one of Clark Kent's less guarded remarks about fish'n'chips "shacks": "Stale chips and haddock that taste of nothing. You might as well eat the fat-sodden paper plate too. The stupid Brits would fry up their slippers given half a chance. What muck!"

Very interesting: the chicken barons versus the venerable British fishing fleet, and I was doing their dirty work for them. So the "chicken meat consortium" was no phantom, no fantasy dreamt up by some crazy master-spy.

The evening would end somewhat differently than originally planned. At the very least, it would not end so quickly.

"This Tandoori muck," Paddy had managed to talk himself into a rage, "it seems impossible, but did you know even Harrods delivers this stuff? But what would you expect, Harrods is no longer British. And then this fenugreek powder." He shuddered. "A mishmash of everything, fried, cooked, acrid, creamy, smoky, fruity, crispy and salty, all at the same time. Yummy. I could throw up."

He shook himself, and calmed down. "Oh well, what the hell. I'll get us another beer, for old times' sake. And then I have to unpack and go to bed. I have an appointment with MI5 at noon tomorrow, just round the corner here. They have a plan. A really cool little number it'll be. You'll see, Debbie Collins, you'll see." He stretched. "It's nice talking to you again. Do you remember when we did it on top of the warm pizza oven in the canteen at HQ? Those were hot times." He grinned and disappeared towards the bar.

I nodded imperceptibly, and vaguely recalled one of those MI5 types, who used to hang around the pubs at HQ in the evenings, on the lookout for "fresh meat" for their allegedly so lonely nights. He was an unsavory character from Whitby way, who considered himself particularly irresistible.

I watched Paddy go. O'Brien had obviously not noticed that I was on the verge of becoming sentimental and was thinking about those three freckles. For whatever reason, I wanted to go to bed with him. Of course, it was partly for old times' sake. And because I needed a bit of tenderness. In the end, I was a woman, and over 40 to boot. There were no longer that many opportunities for "tandoori nights" on any kind of oven.

On the other hand, I still had a job to do. I struggled with the thought and suppressed a belch. I shouldn't have had that last pint. Damn it. Why did my sense of duty have to assert itself right now?

Hesitantly, I shuffled forward on my stool and arched my back. The M1911 pressed uncomfortably into my spine.

I leaned sideways a little and looked out the window and across the street, at the little green shaded by trees, and the weathered stocks where nagging wives had once been imprisoned by their hands and feet.

I had to think.

A place of execution.

I turned away with a sigh. Perhaps it was the sign I had been waiting for. OK, I'd made my decision. A shame that O'Brien obviously had rather different plans for the evening. A single bed rather than an oven-top. It tickled my vanity a little, I must admit, but on the other hand, too much feeling is fatal in my job. No way was I going to screw up this assignment. O'Brien would not be needing his bed anymore.

I raised my glass and made another decision. O'Brien would be my last assignment. I would cash the check, pull out of the trade, and retire. Perhaps I'd even work with Veronica again. Good linguists were always in demand.

I rose and went to stand by Paddy at the bar, perhaps a shade too close.

"I've changed my mind. We should switch to whisky. They serve a particularly good Irish malt here at the Queen's Head."

Paddy nodded and shoved my beer across. "OK, we'll have another one or two. But no more."

So that was that. They found Paddy the next morning at the foot of the old stone cross on the market square. His body contained a magazine-full of bullets from my old pistol.

I often reflect wistfully on those times. There are still fish'n'chips. MI5 never found the Nerd, the murders of Paddy and all the others have never been solved. Neither has the question ever been answered as to why the series of attacks which had suddenly set the whole country in turmoil came to an equally sudden end.

I threw Daddy's pistol into the bay at Cadgwith. That's where I went to settle, and I opened a little B&B, Shiva's Hillside. My guests love my Cornish pasties, the mild Cornish climate, and the musical evenings with my neighbors Paul McMinn and Brian Jenkins, as well as the incomparable view across the cove.

When occasionally the old restlessness and my karma grab hold of me, I can be found early in the morning, even before I've made breakfast for my guests, in an old dinghy that belongs to my pals in the SAS, ploughing through the glistening sea off the cove and racing with the dolphins.

Chateau D'Aigle, Switzerland.

THE WALKING PHILOSOPHER[8]

MARCOS BULCÃO
BRAZIL

8 Excerpt from the book *The Walking Philosopher*. Rights in English available. Contact editor@kbrdigital.com.

Marcos Bulcão has a PhD in Philosophy from the University of São Paulo and does not hide his adventurous nature. Restless and curious, he always sought to meet new people and places, to practice new sports and look for the next adventure. Marcos has lived in more than 30 different places across eight countries, and has practiced rappelling, parachuting, bungee-jumping and trekking. He did the Camino de Santiago in 1998, and was the first Brazilian (and the first traveler from North or South America) to cover the 1,200 miles of the Via Francigena.

He is the author of books and articles on philosophy and psychoanalysis. The Portuguese version of The Walking Philosopher, his first book in non-fiction literature, was published in Brazil in 2014.[9]

*Translated by **Noga Sklar***

---

9 Bulcão, M. (2014). *O Filósofo Peregrino: de Londres a Roma a pé – 2.000km na Via Francígena*. Rio de Janeiro: Record.

Of Socrates and Mr. Hyde,
everybody has a side

There comes a time when we must leave behind our own threadbare clothes, molded in the shape of our bodies, forget the paths that always lead to the same destination. It is time for the journey; and if we do not dare to make it, we will remain forever separated from ourselves.

Fernando Teixeira de Andrade

I've always had an inclination to be "adventurous," for as long as I can remember. As a child, as happens with almost every child, my adventures consisted of climbing roofs and walls, or getting on my bike to explore the adjacent neighborhoods. I sneaked in and out of "forbidden" places, just to feel the rush of "adrenaline" (I hope my mother never reads these lines!).

Nevertheless, this curiosity, this wish to explore new places and sensations, has never left me; on the contrary, it has become stronger with every passing year. From rooftops and trees I moved on to bungee jumping, rappelling and parachuting. When I left the neighborhood, I wanted to see the world; and because of this "restlessness," I had (I still have!) serious difficulties in staying put for too long. Despite spending my first 20 years in no more than two different homes in the same Brazilian city (Salvador), today I have collected more than thirty different addresses in eight countries: Brazil, England, France, the United States, Italy, Spain, Germany, and Canada. This need to move, to be on the move, is part of who I am. I would not know how to live otherwise. With this personality trait, the shifting between projects and places has become second nature.

After graduating in Philosophy (in Sao Paulo) and getting my master's degree in Psychoanalysis (in Paris), I decided to experience the adventure of crossing a country on foot, walking from the French border to Santiago de Compostela, and from there to the Atlantic Ocean, an endeavor that would take me 36 days and a pair of boots.

After that I returned to my studies, this time to earn a doctorate degree, while entertaining the idea of embarking on another big hike. To avoid repeating the Spanish Route to Santiago, I decided to walk from London to Athens as a kind of homage to the cradle of analytic philosophy — my area of expertise — and philosophy in general.

Meanwhile, searching for the best route to take, I discovered another pilgrimage path called the Via Francigena, as ancient but much less famous than the Santiago road. The Frankish Route, or "the road that comes from France," has also been known as the Via Romea, Rome being its main destination.

As a pilgrimage route, Via Francigena dates back to at least the 10th century. Sigeric, the Archbishop of Canterbury, documented his return route from Rome in 990 A.D, after visiting the city to pay tribute to Pope John XV and receive his *pallium* — a white embroidered stole, the symbol of his ordination as Archbishop. Sigeric's diary provides the reference points for this route.

Nevertheless, if we consider Via Francigena as part of the broad, complex Roman road network, we must search for its origins in far more ancient times, about a thousand years earlier. In fact, a road system was built to connect Rome to the province of Britannia after Emperor Claudius led the second Roman invasion of Britain in 43 A.D. Via Francigena was the backbone of this Roman road system at the time, significant for both its commercial and military relevance, since it functioned as the shortest route between Rome and the North Sea. Indeed, unlike other Mediterranean civilizations, which based their development almost solely around harbors, the Romans invested heavily in terrestrial commerce, spurring an unprecedented mercantile expansion across the different regions of the Empire. At its peak, including all the secondary roads of lesser quality, the Roman road network covered approximately 100,000 miles, resulting in the popular expression, "All roads lead to Rome."

With the decline of the Roman Empire, the Protestant Reformation, and other important changes in the geopolitical European scene during the Middle Ages, parts of Via Francigena were abandoned, while other parts were incorporated into local road networks.

Via Francigena was "rediscovered" in 1985, when, after almost a thousand years, the Italian archaeologist Giovanni Caselli recovered and remapped Sigeric's itinerary. Nine years later, the ancient road acquired the status of an "European Cultural Route." The complete path was divided into 80 stages crossing four countries — England, France, Switzerland, and Italy — and covering, approximately 1,200 miles.

I thought this was great. I now had the perfect excuse to travel on a far more organized route than I had previously planned. I would follow Sigeric's path in reverse, leaving Canterbury in direction of Rome. At any rate, if this route did not satisfy me, I could always proceed towards the Parthenon.

Before the Beginning, on the Plane to London

A particular incident with Virginia Woolf comes to mind right now. After a huge effort, weeks of working in vain, and dozens of pages torn out of her notebook, she told her husband that she had finally found the first sentence of her book. Here's the greatest feat! As if the entire book could be contained in that first sentence; as if the wall between the writer and the words had fallen, and all she had to do was to expose them, one after the other.

I envision this scene, and two things occur to me. One is the famous struggle involved in starting to write a book (at least one that does not result in a philosophy thesis): the challenge is related to the fact that a series of possible approaches exist, a variety of stories that could all potentially achieve the desired result. Hence the writer's task, since each set of opening lines would lead to a different outcome. How can one make any such decisions? What makes one story better than another? Or, at least, why does a particular story deserve to be told in the first place?

This issue might sound trivial or even meaningless to most people; but to me it is crucial in more than one aspect, reflecting another important set of questions. How does one choose between different lifestyles, professions, careers, and goals? Should we keep ourselves more adventurous, nomadic, unmarried, living one day at a time? Or instead, should we opt to be settled and bookish, career professionals with wives and children, homes and assets? Or maybe a variation of the above, or a totally different set of possibilities?

These issues might seem silly, and perhaps pertinent to inexperienced teenagers. I am far from being an adolescent, but these kinds of choices are still absolutely crucial to me. These questions need to be addressed, although their answers may feel more like the Holy Grail: something you desperately aim for, but that in essence is unachievable because it is unreal, pure myth.

Anyway, answerable or not, these issues and the attempts to address them are tied directly to the choice of the first sentence of a book. They determine, or at least strongly influence, what comes next in the subsequent text, sometimes to such an extent that we are simply dragged along by the events that follow, as they challenge our ability to predict or anticipate the future. What comes to mind is the now classic *Thelma & Louise*, a movie where a few decisions and isolated events end up sealing the (fatal) destiny of the two main characters.

In other words, we may opt for one or another course of action, one out of many choices — the "sentences" of our personal stories — without any idea of how this decision might affect the whole course of our lives. The possibilities we face may often seem equally good at the time; therefore, we choose one way instead of another without much thought. But we may also fail to consider that these alternative routes do not necessarily follow parallel, or even similar, paths; it is unlikely that we will return and experience another route, telling the story we left behind...

As a matter of fact, writers can always write another book, which might bring them some relief. When it comes to life, however, we do not have another one to live: all we have is here and now, right in front of us. How then can one act or make a decision? The truth is, I don't want to set aside any of my possibilities! I want to lead the life of an adventurer, someone who travels to all possible places, meeting all kinds of people. But I also want the life of a "Borgesian"[10] philosopher, for whom his library is his world, where there are no experiences outside of the book he is reading or writing.

I wish for a stable life with a wife and kids, a career, a readily recognized role in society; yet I cannot give up the nomadic life, the freedom to go wherever I want and whenever I want it, every time the thirst for novelty appears. I don't want to have to justify my actions or the changes I go through, preferring as much anonymity as possible.

From these lines, one can easily grasp of my problem. I mean, some will say that there is no problem at all: "Grow up! That's the answer to your 'unsolvable' enigma!" But since I don't quite see that adults are in a better position, I prefer to keep wondering. My questions may have no answer, I admit, but imagine what one achieves just by trying to answer them.

Therefore, as you might guess, I did the only thing a curious mind could have done: I decided to try. To try and live and get to know everything, without closing any doors; to face all the opportunities and every new experience. I have traveled as much as I could, every way I could, from "luxury tourism" to backpacking. And I've also had my share of settling down, especially during my years in

---

10 "Borgesian" refers to the Argentine writer Jorge Luis Borges and his famous short story "The Library of Babel," which Borges imagines as containing all the books that could ever exist, created from all possible combinations of letters, words, and stories.

college. I'm a "bookworm," but I also enjoy bodybuilding. I can spend days on end with only books for company, but I'm also a fan and an amateur practitioner of various sports. I've crossed Spain on foot, and now I'm planning to walk from London to Rome. Yes, I am a philosopher. And I'm also a walker.

At any rate, as interesting as my life may seem to be — and I think it is — one can't forget the price you have to pay. If it is true that I earned some recognition as a researcher, it is also a fact that I could have done a lot better and published a lot more had I devoted more time and energy to this endeavor. On the other hand, if I had dedicated myself entirely to a life of adventure, I could have possibly won some notoriety for my travels, written a few books, and earned a living.

Nevertheless, no one can have their cake and eat it too, and I know that. Moreover, it is impossible to be an amateur all your life while, at the same time, expecting the recognition deserved by a professional dedicated to his career. This is exactly my problem, my dilemma. I want to love what I do, all the time; and for that, I want to be able to stop and change my activities when I see fit. If, on the one hand, it is true that I'd like to make money through each of my activities, on the other hand, I don't want to be compelled to do things just to earn a living, to work "on commission." I want to desire something, to make a decision, to plan for it, and then do it. And as a result, if I can, to get paid for it. Is it too much to ask, or am I just reclaiming something we are all entitled to?

As to the second thing that came to my mind… I don't remember. Suddenly it occurs to me that these reflections could well be the beginning of the book that I plan to write about this adventure that's about to begin... (without claiming to be Woolfian-like, of course). This is, after all, one of the goals of this travel diary: To write down my thoughts, my fleeting insights, the moment they appear, forcing me into the very act of writing them. Yes, in a way, that's what Via Francigena is: A kind of motive to write about an experience whose intensity will possibly allow me to know my limits in an unprecedented way. That's how perfect this challenge is, a challenge that is mental and physical at the same time. When exhausted by physical and mental demands, the mind requires renewal, reinvention. That's the purpose of this journey through Europe, the major goal of this adventure: To create the ideal conditions in which I will be able — or rather, forced — to reinvent myself.

At this point, I stop and reflect: How pretentious these first lines are! I wonder if I'm already tripping, daydreaming, writing when I should be sleeping. Anyway, it was good to "break the ice," taking away the "burden" of writing the first page, the first chapter. It's all gone now, and I'm ready for the Via Francigena.

1st Stage: Canterbury → Calais (23 Miles)

I woke up at 8:00, feeling renewed and full of expectations. I took a quick shower, had breakfast, and returned to the Cathedral, this time to request the first stamp on my Pilgrim's Credential. It was easy. I identified myself as a pilgrim right at the booth where they sell admission tickets and got the stamp immediately. I was also granted free access to the Cathedral, and found that the building's grandiosity was not restricted to the exterior.

Once inside, catching sight of my backpack, a security guard approached me, inquiring if I was a pilgrim. I said yes, and he asked if I wanted to speak with the priest and have him bless my journey. Yes, why not? Minutes later, Reverend Patrick Goodsell came to see me. He asked me where I planned to go. Rome, I said. A long way, he responded. It takes courage to do something like that. I kept silent. Then he invited me to visit the crypt and St. Mary's chapel, both located in the basement, the oldest part of the Cathedral which is usually closed to the public. I accepted, of course, and was pleased with the privilege. When we left the crypt, very close to the spot where Thomas Becket was murdered, he granted me the special pilgrim's blessing and wished me good luck on my journey. I thanked him, and finally left. It was now 10:00.

On this first day, I faced two major options. One was to sleep on English soil, before reaching Dover, to avoid overexerting myself on the first day of walking. The other was to complete the planned 20 miles to Dover, take the ferry, and sleep in Calais, France. I began walking, having opted for the first choice. I had already experienced overextension on my first day on the Camino de Santiago, and although that had been a truly unforgettable day, it was not something you should plan to do. I looked at the map and went forward, planning to stop over in Sheperdswell, a small village about 10 miles from Canterbury.

A Touch of History: Thomas Becket

Thomas Becket, or Saint Thomas of Canterbury, was Archbishop of Canterbury from 1162 until his murder in 1170 on the orders of King Henry II. Outraged by the fact that the King had been crowned in the Cathedral of York and not in Canterbury, as was historical practice and privilege, Becket excommunicated various opponents within the church, including the archbishops of York and Salisbury and the Bishop of London, who had performed the coronation.

Taking such gestures as acts of treason, Henry sent four horsemen in pursuit of Becket, who was supposed to be called to account. When Becket refused to comply with the orders of the King, the knights delivered him the fatal blows with their swords. Shortly after his death, the faithful began to worship him as a martyr. Becket was canonized by Pope Alexander III only three years after his death.

The route departing from Canterbury was part of an ancient Roman road. The old track is now part of North Downs Way, one of the 15 national trails that cross through some of the finest English landscapes, and I was able to follow it for a few miles. In this part of England, the path basically follows secondary roads, making the route much more interesting than the busy A2.

I hit the road feeling excited, anxious to start the journey and leave the first miles behind. I confess that this state of mind almost made me pass St. Augustine's Abbey without a proper check. But I managed to resist my "athletic impulse," and I was amazed to find the ruins in great condition. Founded in 597 A.D. by Saint Augustine himself, this abbey played a major symbolic role in the revival of Christianity in the South of England, serving as a tomb for the Anglo-Saxon kings of the County of Kent. The abbey is a very important historical and tourist site in the region, although it often goes unnoticed. Although I had already been to Canterbury twice, I had never heard about it. It was a good thing that I was able to make this stop, since it was the high point of this first part of the day. Despite the excitement of being en route, the first miles did not offer much. I had certainly managed to avoid the highway, but even on smaller roads the surrounding landscape did not carry any special interest.

Therefore, I decided to add some "extra excitement" to the walk, and confident in my GPS, I left the road and took a shortcut through the trails that crossed a variety of private farms. With the adrenaline rush, my mood changed completely, and I finally had the impression that the adventure, the real journey, had begun.

All went well for several miles. I didn't even feel the passing of time until the trail I was following led me to a huge plantation, dense enough to stop me from walking through it. Confronted with this obstacle, I could pick a trail to the right or to the left, but, unlike other forks, neither of these led in the right direction. I was worried, of course, that a wrong decision would take me miles out of my way for nothing, something I preferred to avoid, especially on the first day. I also had the option to walk back a mile, to the last access signaling the road. This would ensure my return to the path indicated on the map. But I decided not to go back. I placed my bets and put my chips on the left, walking about a mile until I found a secondary road. I was not very happy when, shortly after, I saw a sign indicating "Barham 3 miles," which meant my adventure through the farms and fields had cost me a few extra miles. I'm not saying it was not worth it, since these miles and their uncertainty gave me the adrenaline rush that I sought for that first day. Anyway, the lesson was learned. GPS can point in the right direction, but there's no guarantee you will be able to follow it... From now on, it would be advisable to use it together with the TopoFrancigena maps.

I arrived in Sheperdswell around 3:30, supposedly my destination for the day. I stopped to rest and eat. The GPS scored about 13 walked miles. It was a beautiful day, and I was full of energy. I just didn't want to stop. I checked my maps and saw there was another stopover in Whitfield, three miles away. I decided to move on. An extra walking hour wouldn't hurt me. However, somewhere along the line, I didn't see the signs for Whitfield and ended up on the busy A2, the opposite of what is known as a pleasant walk. Backtracking was not an option, since I wasn't even sure of where I had gone wrong. Unexpectedly, Dover had become an unavoidable destination, and I regretted not having stayed put in Sheperdswell as planned. Walking along the treacherous A2 roadside, the miles seemed to stretch endlessly; I was bored, and my feet were burning, giving dangerous signs that the day would end with blisters. It would be best to stop at the first available hotel or inn.

After a while, I saw a sign indicating "Whitfield" and the hotel recommended by my guide. I wondered if, in fact, I had taken a wrong turn. It didn't make any difference though. At an unfeasible rate of £105 a day, I was quickly back on the road... growing more and more tired. When I was about 1.2 miles from Dover, I finally found a series of small motels, which I initially hailed as an oasis in the middle of a desert. However, I had to say goodbye to these useless mirages, since they were also out of my reach.

I lost hope for a moment, but the sight of the port of Dover in the distance gave me the courage to proceed. *It would be no more than half an hour*, I thought. Not only would I save some money, but I would be following the recommendations of the official guide as well. Better yet, I would sleep on French soil!

With this in mind, I got to the boat, which is where I am now, legs up, my feet destroyed, just hoping that the damage isn't too great. I have walked 21 miles so far, too much for a first day. History repeats itself. And all I can think of is finding a small inn in Calais, taking a shower, having something to eat, and going to sleep.

THE SUBVERSIVE EFFECTS OF RETIREMENT[11]

ANA CECÍLIA CARVALHO
BRAZIL

11 Excerpt from the book *The Neurotic Cook Book.*

Ana Cecilia Carvalho has a degree in Psychology from the Federal University of Minas Gerais, a Master Degree in Psychology from the U.S. International University and a PhD in Comparative Literature from the Federal University of Minas Gerais. She has worked in the field of Psychology and Literature with emphasis in Psychoanalysis and Literature, and is the author of *The Poetics of Suicide in Sylvia Plath* and *The Neurotic Cook Book*. Ana lives in Austin, Texas.

*Translated by **Hal Reames***

I never imagined wanting to retire. I couldn't understand how a retiring professor could look ecstatic as he walked out the door. To me, retirement meant the end of my interactions with students. What could be more rewarding than the privilege of taking part in their growth, at least those who had a thirst for knowledge? I thought I would even miss the obstinate ones who resisted learning. How would I replace the classroom as a source of renewal and personal growth? If I left, I would disappear from their memories. What importance would I have? It felt worse than dying.

The most important factor in my decision to retire involved Austin, Texas, my husband's hometown. If I limited myself to traveling during school holidays, I would either be without him, or he would spend nine to ten months per year separated from his family in Austin. My husband did not put undue pressure on me to retire from teaching, but he did take me to visit some wonderful friends in Potomac, Maryland. While standing in front of their fireplace, listening to the crackling of a fire on a cold January night, we talked about having the time to travel to such places. Then, we returned to Austin, where his three loving grandchildren hugged their Grampa and Gramma. Soon after our arrival, we stopped at Antone's and listened to the piano blues of Marcia Ball and Pinetop Perkins. By the time Ball's guitarist finished his solo, I'd decided I would sign my retirement application as soon as I got back to Brazil.

What changed in my life with this decision? Nothing right away. Before beginning to taste this freedom, I had to confront some ghosts, among them, the old Jewish guilt which descended upon me every morning. I no longer awoke at 6:00 am, but I was too guilty to sleep past 8:00. I no longer had to jump up running, hurry to my car, then drive disgruntled to campus through the center of a city of almost four million. I could page calmly through the paper while having breakfast. But the guilt persecuted me:

"How can you just sit there having breakfast instead of doing something useful? Start an article! Do a review! Write a book!"

Worse were the retirement paydays. Despite the pittance I received, whenever I would make a withdrawal, the voice of guilt screamed in my ear, "Aren't you ashamed to get paid for doing nothing?!"

In self-defense, I reminded myself of all I had done for more than thirty years. Yelling back at my superego, I tried this argument: "In Brazil, no prisoner spends more than thirty years in prison for any crime!"

Happily, this period of self-flagellation passed. And, to be honest, it passed quickly, giving way to happier and more carefree times. Soon, everything had changed, and for the better. Now I knew why my retiring colleagues looked so happy. It came from having the free time to do whatever they wanted to do while they still had their health and energy. I began to feel free and, more importantly, deserving of this freedom. Finally, I could do what I wanted, make my own schedule, and read and write without worrying about goals, expectations, and demands.

What I discovered next surprised me. One day my husband needed a bibliographical reference from the bookcases of our library. At that moment, I realized that I had misplaced something more than just a book on psychoanalysis. I had lost my interest in teaching the subject. I realized that for months I hadn't even entered that room, once referred to by my children as "Mom's Production Central."

He looked deep into my soul, and saw my irritation and tedium as I looked for the book. Discrete as always, he didn't say anything at the time. Only much later, when I was paging through a cooking magazine while watching Nigella Lawson on TV, he made his point in a manner somewhere between paying me a compliment and provoking me. He showed me that I was free to pursue an area of interest other than psychology, saying, "Analysis and cooking, it is only to start."

I had to admit he touched a nerve with this observation. Half angry, I projected my own self-recrimination onto him, despite being psychoanalytically trained not to do such things: "What are you trying to say, that I don't have the right to waste time?"

Rebuffing the critic's role that I had tried to thrust upon him, he responded, "Who said that cooking is a waste of time? Not me. I would love to cook if I could create what you do in the kitchen. I am only saying that maybe you should consider spending your time on something which gives you so much pleasure."

Now, both flattered and provoked, I searched for an answer; but he took me off the hook by asking, "Is there still a piece of that apple pie you made yesterday?"

I always liked to cook, even when I was occupied with teaching, writing literary and academic works, seeing patients, and attending to family obligations. Retirement from the university permitted me to move away from an identity I'd constructed over many years. Thus, this book represents a subversive act, diverting the path of my identity from psychologist to cook, to cooking not as a retreat but as an act of love.

The Argentinean writer, Jorge Luis Borges, questioned the very concept of authorship. He believed that the world of literature was a vast expanse of quotations available to any writer. I believe something similar happens in the world of cooking, where it is very difficult to assign ownership to a recipe. So, many recipes presented in *The Neurotic Cook Book* are the result of my own appropriation, my interpretation, so to speak, of the recipes of others. I truly hope that these recipes, as they are passed along to others, never reach the point of inertia and repetition which is typical of neurosis.

HAPPINESS IS AN ECSTATIC MOMENT[12]

NOGA SKLAR
UNITED STATES

---

12 Excerpt from the novel *No Degress of Separation*. Rights in English available. Contact editor@kbrdigital.com. The title of this piece is a reference to a quote by Yoko Ono: "I relate to happiness as an ecstatic moment — something you don't create, you encounter."

Noga Sklar was born in Tiberias, Israel, in 1952. She grew up in Belo Horizonte, Minas Gerais, and lived for 30 years in Rio de Janeiro, Brazil. She now lives in Greenville, South Carolina, where she works as a writer and chief-editor with KBR. Noga graduated in architecture from Universidade Santa Úrsula, Rio de Janeiro, but in her youth was better known as a furniture designer and graphic artist. She started to dedicate herself to literature after publishing her first book, in the year 2000 — *Fases da Lua*, by Editora Madras, republished later by KBR as *Eu, xamã* — in which she recounts her experiences as a shaman and a New Age activist. It was the beginning of her original style, "self-radiography," better advertised as "autobiographical fiction," a genre she practices still today. Her first book published in English is *Welcome to America* (KBR, 2016).

I fell asleep before 8, and now at 4, I am fully awake, worn out, in a spin. While he was sleeping, we took a long bike ride together into the morning breeze — at the seashore in St. Aug. a splendid, passionate, ageless couple blessed by the reflection of the sun in their silvery curls... wow. Quantum love, quantum time, our two ubiquitous selves, particle and wave, strings of swirling energy vibrating in cyberspace. He reminds me of the good things in life, the pleasures I left aside a long time ago, a shift in my previous desire to simply give up and die. Do you remember Pina Bausch, my love? We talked about her the other day, and I just realized she's in New York right now with her company, a new season... amazing! Even locked in my cage, I keep in touch. I had great fun with the description of the show, which includes a dialogue more or less like this:

(A couple on stage, with a strong foreign accent)

"Do you think I have an accent?" she asks, reinforcing the obvious. "Can I love you for a day?"
And he categorically: "No".
"Can I love you for a minute?"
"Nooo."
"Can I love you for 30 seconds?" (A last-ditch attempt.)
"Okay," he reconciles. "You can, but just for 30 seconds."
(She starts kissing him, while he watches his stopwatch.)
"Are you going to count the time?"
Hey, Alan. You make me feel like dancing. Can I love you for the

rest of my life? You make me feel like dancing, like singing, all the time. You make me feel like smiling, like living... ALL THE TIME — that's another good reason why I love you so much.

"I'm arrived, my dear. Lovely notes to wake my day. You become brighter with each email you write."

"Hello, my dear. Same here, I have received the same message six times. I was thrilled with seven emails… life is becoming brighter."

"Really? What a system."

"You know, I think about you all day, so I keep collecting thoughts to tell you when we get together, like Pina today, a funny story. A few years ago, just imagine, I was lucky enough to meet her here in Rio, a simple, strong woman, *merveilleuse, wunderbar*. I even asked her for an autograph. Yes, I did, as I was a fan. I worked for her as an interpreter, and it was too much of an honor, let me tell you."

"*Parle a moi*, yes, with you it's like having the sun inside, Noga, and how kind you are, even capable of songs, infinite lovely light."

"I had this bar in Rio called The Grail, where we used to show videos of her Tanztheater Wuppertal… such as the expressive 'The Man I Love,' in which a tall guy, huge hands, interpreted the lyrics in sign language, while in the background an old scratched record of an old woman singing in a crooked voice was playing. Moment, honey, phone."

"So, as they watched, my waiters learned the gestures and kept singing 'The Man I Love' silently with their hands, not a sound... It was so beautiful. I told Pina the whole story, wow. I would love to share it with you but I lost the tape, *dommage*. The Grail was actually an interesting place, kind of half-destroyed, Gothic atmosphere, very avant-garde. There were also theater performances in which the actors walked around the bar almost naked... all this back in 1986. It was a hit with the 'people that counted'... Until one night, during a Halloween party, the neighbors complained about the noise, and the cops came and took away our stereo, end of story. I gave up, closed up shop."

"Fascists... I would expect nothing else... in 1986 I was in Waikiki."

"But wait, the drama did not end yet. Almost a year later, my intercom rang and the doorman (sounding really happy, the man always thought I was trouble, I almost spelled 'doormat') announced the cops were asking for me. I got a bit anxious, but all they wanted was to return my old, lousy stereo… which I exchanged shortly after for a bottle of champagne. Pain today, pleasure tomorrow."

"Good karma, Noga, *à votre santé*! How's your mother doing?"

"Uhh, not good. I left early this morning to go to the bank, and left her a note with the blessed tranquilizer that she hates and the newspaper opened on the article about Pina, whom she also admires. She pretended she did not see the small pill… so when I came back, catastrophe… such a struggle, dear."

"Grind it up in some juice… More specifically, how did she deal with the help?"

"In fact, our long-time cleaning lady will replace me while I'm out of the country, poor thing… I thought it would do some good if she had an idea of what awaits her."

"How was it that you knew the lyrics to Jobim's 'Corcovado' with such elegance?"

"It's an old song, everyone does."

"*Pas moi.*"

"Well, dear, you're a gringo!"

"Gringo?"

"Yes, an American foreigner. Don't you speak any Spanish at all?"

"I know what *gringo* is… not a term of endearment in L.A."

"Yes, correct, but the foreigner will be me, right? You will be home as usual. Listen. I keep dreaming, making plans… dream precedes reality. If we so decide… in less than two months I'll be ready to move."

"Big PLANS… it is so odd to be thought of as a foreigner… I don't feel like one, *je suis un homme de terre*, no divisions."

"All's well, running smoothly. The baby is coming… natural, easy delivery, open paths. Your laser scalpel at work."

"A much expected child, this love of ours. Out of time… dynamic, healthily alive. You bring me joy, Noga, more life to my life."

"Do you think I'm rushing? Anyway, that's my style, what else can I do? I take full responsibility for my own dreams."

"We share the dream. I'm not worried. You are so sane; it is delightful to see a healthy human being."

"We both had, in a way, this symbolic death wish... Now this is another death we've managed to beat. Our souls are redeemed when we surrender without reservation: *la petite morte*, aka orgasm."

"Your orgasm, Noga, yes, I would like to see that. I'm always fascinated with the orgasmic, the beatific, yes, fascinated with your orgasm."

"Minute, dear. Be right back."

"?"

"I went to the bathroom, the body is real, urgent. You would like that? That's what you said? Well, you're going to have so much of it, it will make you sick. My orgasm, I mean… Our... Yes, what? I have no words to describe it. Thrilling? Awesome? Most splendorous thing?"

"Yes, ours. Coming together. I like splendorous. I shudddder."

"Oh, wow. Aurora borealis."

"Let me hold you embrace you awaken you slowly, Noga... Caress your back with open hand gentle fingers. Feel the warmth of you, you move me so. Come. Sit on my lap."

"I'm already there, darling, since you came in... Deep sigh. I wish I were asleep... No part of me is asleep, head and hurt and cunt and all, I mean heart. I know you by heart. Now, Alan, tell me: how large are your hands?"

"I have good hands, long fingers. Intelligent hands. Touch is everything."

"Oh, my God, *tu as raison*, even this man's hands are intelligent... Touch me with your wise hands."

"I know you have a smart cunt."

"What? Smart? Dumb, dense, one thought only. Obsessive, you mean."

"I touch your right breast, as my left hand, being the smartest, unbuttons your blouse. The lovely little breast revealed in sunlight, a small volume, heavy when I hold it, pendulous. I love the arc of it, pink and full, surrounded by color."

"What delight... the smart hand holds my breast, rouses my nipples... erect, easily hardened by your touch... but Alan… why the left?"

"I'm ambidextrous... the left hand being stronger, while the right plays extraordinarily complex arpeggios on the guitar."

"Ambidextrous! Are you human, after all? Or some god, fallen from Olympia?"

"Just a man."

"Ah, no, not just… wrong term. All humans should be like this, but they seemed to have lost their way... You delight me. I'm daydreaming."

"Right. Healthy human male. Evolved. An adult."

I nibble your lips testing your strong teeth, tongue slowly sticks (what a sweet, warm mouth you have). My open palm on your erect breast, the back of my hand travels along your bosom's curve, pink orb on celestial moon, breathlessly alive (I stroke your hair, my eyes shut... can no longer type... if we were together, I would just sit still, feasting from you in quiet adoration). *Your left breast, sister to the right, has to be kissed... the fingertip testing its form, its nipple in my mouth I suck it pink-erect hard. Across the smooth-skinned belly, the bold hand advances, beating around the mound, silky pubic curls…*

"Oh, Alan, it hurts me so to leave you now... but the messenger from the travel agency is here to fetch a check... ten minutes at the most, will you wait online?"

"Hi. I'm back. Sorry I cut you off. Hey, Alan, the nipple's still hard. Hey! Alan!"

"Still hard, come sit on my lap, curls apart I reach inside."

"Reading the screen to check where we stopped. Venus and Mars in joy united, and I'm so wet..."

...I softly stroke your wet labia, tracing fingers reaching for your slit, a slug marking its humid trail tumescent, Alan. *I unzip, slip out my hard erect cock to confront you,* yes, thick and veined, *clothes off, stretched in bed... I land on you,* your nice body, heavy on my hips, *my chest pressing, our hands clasped, lips imprisoned, my cock locked*

inside a throbbing, sucking cunt, should I come now, Noga? My tongue intertwined with yours, no, not yet, *you grab me I stiffen.* I'm shaking, *arms locked in tight embrace, orgasmatically...*

"To me, you are more than real, dear... you are super real... ultra-real. A true blessing, in my room, in my body, in my mouth. In my heart and cunt."

"Yes, and what bliss you are to me... To speak and be understood, without further explanation."

"Now tell me, Alan, is 'cunt' a dirty word? Vagina being so solemnly ugly?"

"Cunt is literary... in erotic literature, the word cunt has no replacement, all the other words being corny... it literally means furrow it is a Saxon word, the image of cunt and cock is certainly Shakespearean. In contemporary parlance in America, if you call a woman a cunt it is the worst thing … It is a powerful word. In England, the word cunt means a stupid woman, an ass, nothing but a problem. But in erotic literature there is no other word to express the fundamental nature of the conjugal relationship. It holds rural imagery, ancestral, the sowing of the land, not basic but idyllic... Of the woods, of the field... Innocent... A powerful word, not corrupted by mechanistic pre-determinism."

"It sounds powerful, yes, but are you sure, Alan, about the literary? Such a strong and original sound in one word, or rather two: cunt and cock, cock in cunt. I understand. The two of us beyond any pre-determinism... And if we decide to publish?"

"If we did it would be erotic, linguistically sophisticated, contemporary, true... without artifice. If you read Chaucer, he speaks with a palate of French... and Jute. We will certainly find cunt and cock in the *Canterbury Tales*. These words are Germanic in nature… When France conquered England in 1066, the language of power was French, and it conquered the native language. Anglo and Saxon were forgotten, relegated to the common folk."

"And retrieved later? Where is the French in the English language?"

"We are trying to find a point in a river, but we cannot... Though quantum physics is more of where we are with 21st century technology. Mechanistic pre-determinism features the physics of the 1800s and 1900s... In the 2000s, reality is what you can perceive with your senses. The 17th through the 20th were centuries in love with science, with knowledge... of cities and the mechanics of automobiles and factories... The enslaving of the soul of man by the mind of man. The philosophy of the senses is idyllic. It transcends the mind. But as a reaction to the end of an era, it is a dead pursuit. Yes, you wanted to know if cunt was a 'bad' word. It is just a word; its meaning is given by whoever is witnessing."

"When the quantum appears things get more personal, endowed with a deeper feeling, somewhat magical again... beyond ordinary senses. To our present standards, Newton's mind might seem pretty narrow... maybe even Einstein's, for the future of knowledge. It does not mean we have seen everything... what a serious talk that began with cunt and cock!"

"Yes, let us speak of coming orgasming of cunt and cock of babies and love. Of the rebirth of life... of art of sanity... of joy, of God, of bliss, of that which is eternal."

"Of music and hope, in brief, let's speak of us."

"Of *Toi* and *Moi*."

"Who typed first, huh? *Ani ve atah neshane et haolam...* you and I will change the world, say the lyrics in Hebrew. We are very poerful together. Oops, powerful, the W had jumped out, full of strength, strong enough to create a life of its own."

"There's an extraordinary, rare energy between us. That's what love is meant to be."

"Right. Until I found you, all I had experienced was an insignificant sample, Alan, *hors d'oeuvres* to increase my appetite... to make me salivate. How do you say this in English?"

"Salivate. I have wakened Noga, and now she's hungry."

"Hungry for you, dear, for everything else, anorexic. My cunt is counting the days until it meets your cock, swallowing it virtually in the meantime."

"And I'm hungry for you. Yes! And in Portuguese, how do you say it?"

"Virtually engulfing you, Alan, how do you say what?"

"Cunt and cock."

"No beautiful words... for cock I have used *pau*, as in 'stick'. Weird, isn't it? Considering the wooden nature involved. I once wrote '*Ser mulher, ter útero e não ter pau,*' to have a uterus not a cock, now that's a woman. For cunt it's even worse, you could say *xoxota* but it sounds terrible, terribly rude, too much for my taste. I would have find it impossible to write erotic poetry in Port, that's why it feels liberating to make love in English."

"Everything has to be disguised. We speak with the passion of Shakespearean England, the language, the rhythm."

"Rhythm is so essential, isn't it? It sets the tone of the prose, the poetic prose, even when we are coming. Or fucking."

"'Fucking' is an Anglo-Saxon term; it also means planting, another metaphor from the English countryside. English is not the ideal language for novels, although it is shaped by them."

"But I'm proving it's just the opposite... sometimes I worry... am I being crass? Because, you know, I'm the freshman here in this form of art."

"Not vulgar, no... deliciously passionate. Poetic. Sex is usually rude, something we shouldn't be talking about."

"Ah, now *je suis tranquille*. And what do you mean by 'rude'?"

"Crass, libertine... inappropriate."

"And before, did you enjoy talking about sex?"

"Oh, no… not at all, Noga. It's not something I have ever written about. It is a new medium for me."

"I see. The other day, you complained I was being rude, I didn't get it... 'Blow job' is a contemporary expression, truly obscene, now I completely understand your *fellatio*, my prince. I apologize. I hadn't realized how literary our conversations were, despite having embarked on them with pleasure and grace. And then things flowed."

"Yes, set sail. A poetic way of speaking. How could it be otherwise? Poetry is never vulgar or crass. Yes... wet enough to sail this ship of thought."

"I feel more enlightened than ever before. Free. Bolder still. My consciousness is expanding, and growing, forming a rainbow over your head... with you, even poetry must be wet... I believe this kind of linguistic retrieval is in the mass subconscious right now."

"Knowing what you know is the beginning of knowledge. And knowing what you don't know the beginning of wisdom... I love your wetness... What an inspirational afternoon, thought making body manifest. What do you mean by 'retrieval'?"

"From the shamanic viewpoint, the recovery of a lost soul. I've just read about it on the blog of a former friend of mine, a well-known theater director from Brazil, also a Jew... the subject was the same, although maculated by a certain degree of vanity."

"What is 'maculated'?"

"Um... I just looked it up in the dictionary, honey. It means 'polluting,' making something dirty. Anyway... What I meant to mention was this need to go deeper into our humanity, our beast-like selves, poetic beasts though. To be idyllic, one has to be fresh, innocent, without fetish... It is an ancient theme, a possible reaction to the overexposure of the body... and yet delightfully sexual, expressing yourself through the pussy... directly from the source. We were born of an orgasm, no doubt about it... or at least, we should have been. The ones lucky enough to have originated from pleasure grow up differently, I believe."

"Yes, orgasm is a kind of re-centering, a rebirth of the self. You must be your self to become yourself... Of course, you are yourself in the first place, albeit slightly confused given the circumstances. The rhythm of the mind traces literary history, the poetic beast man, the noble savage by Rousseau. If we were together, we would do very little erotic writing. The chicken..."

"I totally agree, but I'm having so much fun... go to the library right now, my love, while I sit here at home, okay? I must finish this novel we have already promised to the editor... But first, you must tell me: the chicken or the egg? Alright, thanks for answering before I asked."

"...comes from the egg, Noga. So the egg came first."

"Okay, but in the beginning... there comes creationism, *bereshit* God created..."

"On the fifth day. I taught my children that God was like gravity, sort of always was, has caused everything… and there came an egg, and from this egg came a chicken and henceforth… all chickens came from eggs and chicken eggs from chickens."

"Considering what we already know, the future seems optimistic… about this concept of God, I don't know… I think it was more like the primordial soup…"

"Yes, the form of the primordial soup takes was dictated by gravity, a fundamental part of the soup. What do you mean by future? We take present knowledge for granted… Knowledge transcends time."

"Ay, Alan, I stopped in the middle of the sentence, that's why… I meant to say the future goes beyond what we already know. It's a basis for progress… as in the egg and the chicken… Let's make an omelet and leave the chicken alone. When necessary (to transmit knowledge), the appropriate language appears. Words cannot discover anything, you know, back to not (egg) new… we simply create new words, altered descriptions of reality. Antique thoughts in more contemporary language."

"When the bomb was detonated, no one had seen it before. I love that about you, that I can drift in language and thoughts, and come to the same oasis with you at Ein Gedi."

"What a terrible image… the mushroom, of course, not the oasis in the Negev."

"I know, harsh images, the camps et al… like those hideous postcards for sale in Tahiti, filthy things floating, rising above the pristine Pacific…"

"It truly maculates the beauty, Alan, I love the desert, you know? In 1970, I spent 11 days in the Sinai, no sweet water and no canteen… taste gets numb, no comfort in sight… the beautiful undulating black hills."

"Sweet water, my God, how I love sweet water… Ein Gedi is one of my favorite places on earth, such life from such parched earth, sky, sun, horizon… no crap. Were you lost? Naked?"

"No! Alan! That was the idea; an adventurous, exciting trip in the desert... ecstasy from water, *maim besasson*, get it? We both naked under the palm trees... reborn out of love."

"Come and have dinner with me tonight, Noga, there are salads everywhere... Let me put my arm around your waist and walk with you. Do you want to live here in St. Augustine?"

"I want to live with you, dear, wherever it is... I'm ready to emigrate… To St. Aug, if it is the case, because you already live there. Artsy fartsy as you said sounds appealing, and we are home already since we found each other."

"Let me make my home between your legs, Noga, in your arms in your heart in your mind in your eyes and smile. I will give thought to where we would live here."

"Nice dream, huh… Look, Alan, how's your afternoon going? I could stop for a couple of hours… Can we type again later?"

"I'm delighted with you, Noga... pleased... The librarian has told me I should be leaving... I'll see what I can do, probably… *À tout à l'heure, mon amour.*"

"Ha, we are so synchronized here... love you, Alan. Bye."

Two hours later he was back online, "Hello, *êtes-vous là*?"

I had connected that very moment, "Yes, dear, I'm right here... Where did you go? What did you do? In the last hour, I mean …"

"*Parfait*," he said, "just hold me, Noga... nothing special."

I insist... I type the question again, careful not to miss a key. He ends up confessing, "I bought a *bouteille de vin.*"

I can see where this is going. I'll be back to drinking, moderately this time, I hope.

"Went back to *chez moi*," he continues, "had a glass of wine... listened to National Public Radio. Sought the news of the day, and the news was Noga." He keeps talking, "I fasted for ten days once. Food became an absurdity."

Me too, I have told him before. I was so weak, willing to die. He found the description interesting... "Along with the vow of silence," he said, "it is quite amusing how much is said nonsensically. So now is now. We have courted the razor's edge and I prefer the slit between your legs."

I would love to cook for him, sensory food, not sexy... artistic, sumptuous food (he once said, "Cook away, food is good"). Prepared with love, with feeling. Vegetarian food, but still gourmet. "Food is food," he said, but I disagreed: Food is consciousness. Considering how much I have created, loving and writing since we have met, imagine what I'll be able to create in the kitchen, in the middle of a day dedicated to lovemaking. But he insists, no, it is consciousness that results from food.

Two Chimpanzees[13]

Marcelo Mirisola
Brazil

13 Excerpt from the novel *Joana Against My Will*.

Marcelo Mirisola is considered one of the biggest revelations in the Brazilian Literature of the 1990s. He graduated from Law School, but never became a lawyer. He is known for his innovative and daring style, and the sometimes virulent way he reacts against the *status quo* and the "fraternities" of the literary world. He has also written *Funk, The Returned Hero*, *Bungalow* and *The Blue Of The Deceased Son*. *Joana Against My Will* is his first novel translated to English.

Translated by **Fal Azevedo**

To my missing daughter.

I fucked Joana five times without a condom, which made me feel proud and flattered—at first, more because of the quantity than of any emotional closeness. If only I hadn't made the stupid mistake of wanting to love her at the same time.

This kind of situation that happened three weeks ago, before I got the first email, was inconceivable and totally unlike me. "There goes my ass," I thought.

I don't know if I'm still the same lonely guy now as I was before, fiercely against the mammalian instincts of human beings. After all that has happened, I don't know. My friend Reinaldo Moraes once told me: "One day, you'll come inside the woman who loves you." Maybe some variation of that prophecy had come true. Or had I come inside a hole that loved me?

Is Joana the hole where I've now buried myself? Is that all?

I don't know, I don't know. Maybe I'm just "being melodramatic". Well, there are two things of which I am certain: I left my sperm inside of her, together with all these doubts, and, for one night, Joana freed me from the sentimental misery of the past forty years. Oh God.

The next morning, she refused to answer my call. She told me to call her some other day.

I understood something else. Besides freeing me from the sentimental misery of forty years, she had killed our child with the morning-after pill. She was sleepy. For the first time, someone other than me and my loneliness managed to kill something that had been half-created inside of me. It wasn't fiction. I decided to insist. She deserved it. So did I. Sooner or later, Joana would answer. Of course she would, and when she did, for the first time in those domestic circumstances, I would love a woman as though I was really fucking her.

I knew it wouldn't be easy for Joana to get rid of the half of me that was inside her. I could bet. I had Viagra on my side and a whole procession of dead souls in the graveyards (most call them books; it makes no difference to me) that I had published and that she so admired. It was such foolishness. If Joana would only answer my calls or incorporate the fictional demon with open legs, saying, "That's the way you wanted it, so eat me out now." That was exactly the way I wanted it.

Without a doubt, Joana was the best missionary position experience of my life. She had the softest, roundest ass I'd ever known, and a tongue that always worked in circular, spiraling motions. Those motions were great for both a tentative kiss (I'll talk more about the kiss later) and for oral sex. The latter was surprisingly better than the missionary position. While I can't say we understood each other, it would be unfair to Joana's tongue and the small flaw in her teeth to say that we didn't. The blow job had other advantages – an *à la carte* pussy, and Joana all around it.

So, we fucked. And it was amazing. And she didn't come, and told me the problem was hers. I was head over heels.

Joana was waxed, the old-fashioned way. "Just for you, my love," she said. "Just for me!"

Oh my God, the kiss. Joana entered that motel room like a blind woman, beautiful and hesitant. She licked me diagonally trying to find, something that wasn't there. She surrounded me with a kiss that didn't exist (one that I am still trying to understand). The kiss both pulled me closer to and pushed her away from that uncertain place—that "licked spot." I was swept away and I wanted to know if Joana was "real" and she answered me with her straight hair, not even trying to distinguish "truth" from "lie" since she was my invention, my unfolding that kept running away from me. I couldn't even reach her tongue. But the pull was too strong and we took our excitement and our misunderstandings to bed. She wouldn't look me in the eyes not because she was blind. I understand now it was because I was responsible for the kiss that never was, and Joana, as we had previously arranged, was drunk on whiskey. "I'll be waiting for you at midnight, my love, at the motel, drunk on whiskey, my love." I had to take her undoings and mine (never ours together) to the limit, and that meant I had to tear off her black panties and shove my dick inside of her and try, even though I knew something was wrong about it, to kiss her and fuck her at the same time. I had to forget my machinations and focus only on the sperm that I would pour inside of her. I could make some sort of exchange, killing the fiction and taking "the real woman" in my arms. But if we had anything in common, it was only vertigo, and the vertigo, despite being equivalent, wasn't a collusion. There was actually some imbalance as she tried to dodge my movements, either pretending or trying to believe in herself. I kept thrusting, still thinking I had "the real woman" in my arms.

The situation didn't allow for retreating. So, I can't understand after all that had happened, how she could turn away, or how she didn't suffer from the same loneliness that I did. If she was simultaneously the repository of all of my love and the fruit of all my curses and prayers, then how could she have walked away? Hadn't I invented her? Yes, me, with my own spunk, believing for the first time in my life that I had gotten rid of all my sarcasm and indifference and that "sperm" and "spunk" were the same thing I mean I wasn't there, in that second-class motel room to write another book. I was there to get her pregnant and dodge the death inside of her (even my selfish self said yes), as if reality could challenge the giant and be greater than my internal fire, divided only between us, two chimpanzees, Joana and me, a reality separated from talent and larger than damnation. Why not?

Could Joana have been aware of both the disgrace and the greatness that our fucking might produce? I suspect that perhaps she preferred to ignore what I decided to call "the curse that contains the whole miracle." Or perhaps it wasn't her time. Perhaps she'd had some kind of distorted perception, running away from the kiss, as if she could sense the abyss, seeking some defense from herself and my creation. It made no difference. Everything was a spiraling mix of excitement, hesitant kisses and Rio de Janeiro, and Joana had nothing to do with any of it! After all, I was the one who involved her in that story and climaxed, completely alone, in the most pathetic, predictable way inside of her womb. What had she done? Well, I believed that she did what had to be done. No more and no less than excluding me and the little Indian, my daughter, that she killed with the morning-after pill. If I were Joana, I'd have done the same, even if by instinct alone. .

So, we tacitly shared creation, abortion and a love that wouldn't survive the attraction or the morning after; it would die even before the flesh became rotten or fecund. It was all the same. The guilt and the spunk, however, were all mine. I didn't want to scorn Joana because she took care of it herself. She's a lunatic, a daughter of the abyss, inevitable as the morning after death. No, I won't do that (for now, Hell is all mine). Shit! I was the one who created her. I was the one who had given her the abyss. It had all been my fault. I filled Joana with my sperm to save myself (myself, my God! Not her) from the curse of flying over the abyss, of being the non-tongue, of running away without leaving a phone number or an address. How could she have acted like that?

I would do things my way then.

I shouldn't have been surprised. She followed the proper itinerary that I had ultimately established for myself, the love itinerary, whose last strike is annihilation. It is simply the itinerary that kills some and invents others. The curse lies in a place of perpetual loneliness, the "forever ever after." Only for one night, Joana went through all of the steps. She both killed and died, although she couldn't even suspect nor could have the slightest perception of this when she ran so rightfully from that kiss. The fugitive kiss. That's how the kiss was.

As for fucking, I can say we were in the same condition. At least in the same physical condition, of that I have no doubt. But Joana was taking a greater risk. She could get many diseases and eventually conceive a child, but she still opened herself to me, placing all of her bets on me (on me?). The difference was that I was fucking myself and placing all my bets on us and I believed that Joana was doing the same.

I took my woman as if I had the responsibility of the Holy Ghost to impregnate the Virgin Mary, although I couldn't care less about the long-term result. To me, it didn't matter if the fruit of our passion was Jesus Christ or a retard; what mattered was that we were having "an honest fuck," (at least on my part I can guarantee that) and by fucking that way we could continue on with our lives. There wasn't really another way of fucking; even mice fuck the same way, and they would never know the happiness of escaping from a kiss. We, on the other hand (I believed), knew we weren't mice and that was why we didn't feel the need for "protection," wearing a condom, or taking pills, or checking the calendar. We just had to run away from each other. How could two condemned people protect themselves from "forever?" I had no more and no less than "the curse that contains the whole miracle" or "forever" in my arms. So, it was an honest fuck. My first. Joana behaved like an elliptical lizard. As I thrust more and more violently, I could sense her feet kicking the air, trying desperately to find anchorage on my ribs. That excited me even more, and I tried to reach her stomach with my dick, and moved my body forward with the intention of suffocating her with my shoulders (See what the missionary position can make you do?). If she lost her breath, I imagined she would die in my arms and go straight to heaven at that moment. Joana was focused on making circular movements with her tongue inside my mouth, which confused and excited me and made me pull back and go easy on the thrusts so she could breathe again and kick her feet in the air. I think she did that in self-defense.

Those circular kisses and that spiraling movement that Joana used to lick the base of my shaft have a name, something that resembles a hat. Or something with a brim and a crown that could receive those spiraling licks. It should be said that this "something" was much more than just a blow job. It was both exciting and comforting because it let me fall on my back, resting, after all that thrusting. I don't know if "rest" and "comfort" are the right words, but I know that Joana was working for me and that was only the beginning.

I came to understand her kiss and I knew her teeth. It was as if Joana opened up little by little, or as if she had a vagina in her mouth. With all the nuances, her upper and bottom lips, and the reverberations down there, she had the advantage of a thick tongue that kissed me in spirals (the same way that she sucked my dick). My arms were shaking and I lost my balance a few times, slipping. So I was knocked out and she rode me again. Another specialty of Joana's was that she seemed to become a tongue, licking my body as an invertebrate animal, as though she had the ability to fold herself over, inventing another body for me (like hers). It was as though she could lie on my dick without bending it. We moved backward and forward without really moving, until the moment we separated.

"I didn't come." That was what she told me, lighting a cigarette.

I opened a can of beer, and offered a sip to Joana, who reciprocated with an icy kiss. Very good. The conversation stalled, and I tried to change the tone, or find a way of fixing, through my words, Joana's "mammalian lapse."

"You didn't?" I asked. "That's your problem."

She agreed and laughed. She was the fan, a bedroom mirror, she was myself, something that could fool me and fool itself because of a good story we had invented, a story that, thinking it over, we had taken to an end. Together. Actually (I discovered two days later), Joana knew the fact that our fuck hadn't been as good as my comment, "That's your problem," and that fact would only make the comment true. I mean, you can't fuck only with words, although sometimes this is wiser and necessary. It was curious. On all fours that round ass wasn't that attractive. It was only enchanting. I think I should have slapped that white butt. The problem is I would certainly go about it with too much intensity. I'd never slapped a woman. It's better not to hit, I thought, than to hit too strongly.

But when Joana was on her side, she knew how to ask for a dick, and in that moment I experienced another first. That is, I invested "my dick" in her and occasionally my dick was behind Joana's ass (That ass would accept anything. It could have been a Pataxo Indian or a toucan's beak, whatever). From that point on, I could hold her by her thighs as I'd never done with a woman before. My entire flesh was against her flesh, which always moved in spirals and in the opposite direction. For me, it was the best of all four fucks. Before that, I had sucked her tits, by demand, "Suck, suck my tits," then went into the second phase of that spiraling kiss.

The best moment for Joana, she confessed later, was between the third and the fourth time, when I whispered in her ear, "Open your legs." Well, I don't know now if she "confessed" that or if I had the impression that she did. Despite all of the acrobatics, Joana was my "woman" and she obeyed me. "Open, open your little legs."

In the end, just as we were bridging fiction with reality, the receptionist called, telling us our time was over. I left with a hard-on. I had come five times inside Joana. No, we didn't really fit.

River Kuebe, Menongue, Angola.

BELDADE[14]

FRANCISCO INÁCIO
ANGOLA

—————————
14 Excerpt from the novella *Sex by The River Kuebe*.

Francisco Inácio majored in social communication at the Social Sciences College at Agostinho Neto University and studied print journalism at the Journalist Training Center (Centro de Formação de Jornalistas — CEFOJOR, 2005/2006). He began working as a journalist for the *Angolense* newspaper in 2006, but his first story was published earlier, during an internship at the *Folha 8* newspaper in 2003. He wrote for Africa Today magazine for two and a half years (2007/2008), and also for the *Jornal de Angola*, *Cefojornal* and for *Tveja*, *Marinha*, *PIR* and *Pátria* magazines. He edited the *Indústria* magazine for the Secretary of Industry of Angola and created editorial projects for *Bwefixe!* and *Perfil Biográfico* magazines. He's currently employed as a journalist at the *Jornal de Economia & Finanças* newspaper published by Edições Novembro E.P. Born from his love of writing, *Sex by River Kuebe* is his first foray into the literary world.

Translated by **Amanda Morris**

This is not an endorsement of "travel sex." The goal is to start a conversation on a subject we pretend doesn't happen. Adultery is, therefore, the main theme of this story.

It was a peaceful night on the bank of the Kuebe.[15] The river, a slithery snake, divides Menongue in half. A bridge joins the two sides of the city. The most beautiful area is near the provincial government headquarters, where there is a huge garden with benches and a large screen that airs Angola's public broadcast channels. Young couples in love go there on dates, to enjoy the quiet, comfortable environment, surrounded by flowers and plants that freshen the air and inspire those with poetic flair. But this was not the spot chosen by Pedro. It was too public and constantly watched; he wouldn't get the privacy he needed to achieve his unspoken intentions. He chose to take her to the place where people took baths and washed their clothes, about 300 yards away. He knew those activities took place during the day and, at night, there would be no one there.

They reached the riverbank, still holding hands, at around 9:30pm. As he'd predicted, there was nobody there, but they could hear the sound of animals and the pleasant bubbling melody of water running over the river rocks.

It was a live concert, played by the wonderful and skilled orchestra of nature. Truly, any depressed person would be cured in a few minutes in that harmonious and peaceful environment.

The sky looked angry, jealous of that young outsider's luck. It was sulking, starless and dark, about to cry. Slowly, they walked together to the riverbank.

---

15 The river goes through several municipalities for about 250 miles. It flows into river Kuvango, from its source in the province of Bié.

A huge tree waited for them there, friendly and welcoming. People who'd go there for a swim enjoyed its shadow and rest after a dive in the fresh waters of the Kuebe. It got so strangely peaceful that each of their movements seemed to echo in the depths of the river.

He was the first to speak, pointing to a rock by the tree on which they could sit.

"Ladies first."

She smiled.

"Thank you, sir."

He sat as close as possible to her, to enjoy her body's magnetism. They quietly enjoyed their surroundings, until he finally broke the silence again.

"Do you like this place?"

With a smile, she looked around, and nodded at him.

"Sure!"

"Why? What makes it so special to you?" he insisted.

She gave it some thought.

"It's pretty," was her laconic reply.

"Is that all?"

"Hmm... no!"

"And..."

"I think anyone would like it here. As I said before, it's a good place for a date." She paused, gently poked his nose with her finger and added: "Better yet, to talk. I mean, if you are in good company."

"Are you in good company for a *conversation* right now?" he asked, emphasizing the word "conversation."

"What do you think, or better yet, what do you want me to say?"

"What I want to hear."

They laughed.

"Ok." She looked into his eyes and composedly said: "I'm in good company for..."

"For what?"

"Which one do you like best, a conversation or a date?"

"Aren't they the same thing?"

"They are to me!"

"I choose none. Maybe the latter, if it had a meaning I understood."

"What meaning do you understand?"

"Do you really want to know?"

"This is why I asked."

"For me, a date is a date. You know?" he blurted out.

"No."

"Yes, you do."

"I don't. What do you mean?"

"Maybe, then, the word *dating* is best defined this way: first talking, then hugging, then kissing, then making love."

She laughed hard.

"You've got bad intentions. In what dictionary will I find that definition?"

"I have it right with me if you want to check..."

She glanced around.

"I don't see any dictionaries here."

"It's pocket-sized. I'll show you later." He took a pause, then mumbled, nervously.

"Beldade, my heart is bursting with love and if I can't share it with someone, it might even explode! Boom!!"

She laughed.

"You're funny. But you need to be more romantic, engaging, charming... got it?"

"All paths lead to Rome, my dear. You don't go out with someone just because of the romantic slush they spout. If you liked me, why waste time with inanities? I think we have chemistry..."

She laughed again.

"What makes you say that?"

"When I saw you and when we kissed for the first time, I felt something I hadn't experienced in years. It was as if I'd spent 100 years in jail, never seeing such a beautiful woman as you."

He leaned closer to her and embraced her waist, then told her, in a serious, quiet tone:

"I think I'm falling for you."

"You *think*?"

"Until you tell me that, yes, you feel the same way, I can't be sure of my feelings. It's hard to be loved and not loved in return."

"Then, you can keep your *think*." Disdainfully, she turned her back to him.

He gently held her shoulders, and whispered in her ear.

"Beldade, I'm in love with you. Do you want to be with me?"

She abruptly tore herself away and angrily retorted:

"*Think... be...* what are you saying? You think you impress me? That I'm going to run straight into your arms because you tell me you're in love and you want to be with me? Who do you take me for? Some needy girl who throws herself at the first 'prince' she meets? You know what? I'm out of here!"

She got up and walked away with wide, clumsy steps, not seeing the banana peel on the ground. She slipped, and he ran to her. As if it weren't enough, it started to rain. The sky seemed to be over its jealousy and now laughed at him, so hard it was in tears.

What had started so well was unraveling because of his blunder. He was desperately confused and didn't know where he'd gone wrong.

"I'm sorry, Beldade. I didn't mean to hurt you," he said, while helping her get up. But as soon as she was standing again, she angrily pulled her arm away, shaking off the sand from her clothes.

He realized it was now or never. He had to make her change her mind. He stepped closer.

"Please!" he pleaded. "Believe me, I didn't mean to offend you." He held her gently in his arms. She tried to escape, but he held her tightly, drawing her closer, until they were face to face.

He held her face between his hands, lifted her chin up, looking seriously but gently into her eyes.

"If I said something you didn't like, I deeply apologize. But I want you to know I'm being honest with you. Maybe I should have been more charming or romantic, but... I don't know... it won't stop me from saying what I feel, and I'm in love with you! Whether you want it or not..."

He then kissed her. At first, she tried to resist, but finally yielded to the kiss. She later told him she'd never kissed anyone so passionately or for so long. After that, it all happened very fast.

They exchanged kisses and caresses, slowly dropping to the wet ground. Their bodies, entwined, rolled around the grass, until they reached the huge tree. In the heat and emotion of the moment, he put his hand up her shirt, gently touching her breasts and teasing her nipples, which made her shiver with passion, while she removed his shirt.

The river Kuebe was a silent witness to their kisses, caresses and embraces under the gentle rain, in one of the best expressions of passion: ardent sex bursting into flames of sensation between two bodies dominated by emotion and attraction.

He leaned against the tree, shirtless. His phone rang, but he quickly turned it off without a glance. He was burning up!

She buried her face in his chest, holding him tight. He felt the warmth of her breasts and his penis jerked up, his erection about to poke a hole in his jeans.

She quickly unfastened his pants and grasped his hairy balls. He sighed when she held his dick on her hand and took it out of his pants. He was rock hard.

With her left hand, she stroked his cock and motioned up and down. With the other, opened her bra. She hugged him tightly and smoothly, slowly, sat on his penis, moaning as she felt his warmth deep in her wet pussy.

She repositioned her body, leaning against his, and rode him fast, rode him good, up and down, back and forth, as he held her by the waist and followed her deliciously wanton moves.

Minutes later, they moaned almost at the same time, throwing their heads back and holding each other closer, their semi-naked bodies almost as one. Their voices sounded out, with the typical sounds of a simultaneous orgasm: "Oohhhhhhh... Ahhh! Fuck! This is so hot!"

At a moment like this, obscenities are welcome.

They collapsed, still panting and exhausted. Her t-shirt was bunched over her chest, her breasts exposed; the tender nipples were wet, because he had sucked on them like a baby. They were enveloped by a deep silence, as if surrounded by a mute audience to a porn movie.

He checked the time on his phone. It was almost 10:30pm.

"It's getting late, we'd better leave," he gasped, still out of breath.

She still lay there on his chest. She seemed to have fallen asleep.

"Beldade!" he called, to make sure she was awake.

"Yes, I heard you, I'm getting up," she grudgingly replied.

He walked her home. Before she went inside, he held her hands and kissed her passionately.

"I'll miss you," he said, an expression of sadness on his face.

She was startled, then remembered he was only staying in town for a few days, for work.

She laughed.

"I almost forgot you don't live here! When do you leave?"

"Tomorrow."

This time, she was really surprised and stared at him, angrily.

"Tomorrow? Why didn't you tell me?"

"Yes, tomorrow. I don't know why I didn't tell you... because, hmmm... I forgot. I wish I could stay longer!" her fondled her hands. "I'd love to spend more time with you and get to know you better."

She shrugged, in seeming acceptance, and said:

"Whatever, what else can I say?"

Unexpectedly, as if she'd changed her mind, questions poured out of her mouth, without waiting for an answer.

"So is this the end? Was this just a one-night stand? Didn't it mean anything to you? You mean..." she choked.

"After all you said to me, was it just a game?" she asked, soberly.

He took a while to answer; he feared his reply would hurt her even more.

"Only time can tell. Who knows..."

She said nothing.

When he tried to embrace her, she stepped back. He unsuccessfully attempted a last kiss of solace. Suddenly, she acted unpleasant.

"I leave tomorrow at 10:00. I hope to see you before I go."

"I'd rather not."

"Why?"

"I don't want to see you go!"

She couldn't hide her wet eyes anymore. A tear ran down her face. Before he could comfort her, she turned around, ran inside and slammed the door. He could hear her sobbing.

Pedro was broken-hearted. She was a good girl, but there was nothing he could do. He had to go back to Luanda, no matter what. His whole life, family, friends, job, school, were all there.

On the next morning, he looked out of the plane's window, sad and lost in his thoughts. The plane left the province behind, flying straight through the clouds that would hide it from his view.

Looking down, there was nothing left to say, but a heartfelt, already nostalgic farewell: "Goodbye, Kuando Kubango! It was a pleasure to meet you!" His words were meant for more than one recipient. They were meant for the province and for Beldade, whom he had left behind, sad and lonely. The wing of TAAG's Boeing 737 slid swiftly against the clear sky, white clouds floating on the untouchable and transparent blue mantle. Down below, he left behind a promising province and a heart he had broken.

He couldn't stop thinking about her: her voice, gestures, her beautiful smile, her cordiality and her innocence. He felt guilty. He started to think of the impact sex causes on friendship. He hadn't thought he'd return to Luanda with his heart divided. *Why did I go so far? We could have just talked, remained just friends. Why didn't I just do my job? If I had known...*

His conscience was burdened by all those questions and the resulting guilt. Only then did he remember something he hadn't considered or thought about: he was married and had just cheated on his wife.

His conscience got even heavier.